First Modern
Pennsylvania Academy of the Fine Arts

George E. Thomas

PENNSYLVANIA ACADEMY OF THE FINE ARTS

distributed by

UNIVERSITY OF PENNSYLVANIA PRESS

Foreword
DAVID R. BRIGHAM
7

First Modern: Pennsylvania Academy of the Fine Arts
GEORGE E. THOMAS

Chronology
ISAAC KORNBLATT-STIER
123

Photography Credits
127

Foreword

WHEN THE Pennsylvania Academy of the Fine Arts (PAFA) commissioned Furness & Hewitt to design its new building in 1871, Frank Furness, with whom the stunning structure has become most closely associated, was just thirty-two years old; his partner, George Hewitt, was thirty. As architectural and cultural historian George E. Thomas argues in this volume, while the Victorian ornament and intensity of color dazzle our eyes and inspire the imagination, the true breakthrough of the building is in its innovative use of industrial materials and construction methods that mark the turn toward modern architecture. PAFA's Historic Landmark Building introduced the new possibilities that would lead away from precedent toward the future, not only in its opulence, but also in its skylighted galleries, its new systems of heating and cooling, and in the structurally important and visually impressive truss along Cherry Street (now Lenfest Plaza); this vital element borrows from railroad construction to enable the even north light coveted by artists to be transmitted into the first-floor studio classrooms. Even the decoration within the building modulates between organic motifs, such as flowers, vines, and mushrooms, and industrial elements, from pistons to exposed I-beams and rolled-steel pipes.

When the building was opened in 1876, the Reverend Dr. William Henry Furness, father of the architect, gave the inaugural address. He admitted his bias, but implored the gathered dignitaries to

> *see for yourselves. It is no matter of taste. It is beyond all dispute. No expense has been spared in the endeavor to make this School of the Fine Arts useful and attractive. We all rejoice in beholding*

FRONTISPIECE Revolutionary vs. traditional

PAGES 4–5 Columns made from rolled-steel pipes, ornamented with cast-iron bases and capitals, carry wrought-iron U-channels to span the north transept and the largest public gallery

LEFT The glow of the gallery skylights transmitted to the entrance   7

how munificently its claims have been appreciated. It is one of our oldest Institutions, the earliest of its kind in the country . . . it freely offers all needed aid and instruction to those who devote themselves to the arts of Painting and Sculpture. In a word, its fine office is to breathe the spirit of Beauty into the hearts and dwellings and manners, of men.*

Remarkably, PAFA's Historic Landmark Building works today just as it did on its first day of operation. Visitors enter a relatively compact and dimly lighted foyer that enables their eyes to adjust to the interior, and are then led by the light from above into a soaring grand stair hall that radiates an astonishing array of colors and details in vibrant glass, stone, brass, tile, and gilt-relief panels. The lecture hall and studio classrooms on the first floor remain central to training student-artists from around the world; the galleries on the second floor still benefit the visitor experience through their varying proportions and the ever-changing natural illumination that makes each visit different. Despite the ongoing twentieth-century penchant for white cubes, every contemporary artist who has visited PAFA during my tenure—from Claes Oldenburg to David Lynch and Alyson Shotz—has marveled at the beauty of these galleries and wished to exhibit in their spaces.

The youthful vigor of Frank Furness in 1871 and the dynamic energy of the American Industrial Age are manifested in PAFA's beloved building. This volume marks a new wave of investment in its preservation and the maintenance of its powerful design for the benefit of future generations of artists, schoolchildren, and audiences who come here to seek beauty, knowledge, and inspiration. PAFA is currently engaged in a two-phase Campus Master Plan that includes extensive renovations to the skylights, roof, masonry, windows, elevators, electrical, fire safety, accessibility, art storage, heating and cooling, and other systems. The project begins by addressing the most urgent needs and progresses to take advantage of the latest innovations in historic preservation and building design to ensure that Furness's vision will endure.

We are grateful to the many people who made this volume possible, starting with author George Thomas, whose valuable insights enable us to understand the innovative nature of the building and appreciate its value today at the heart of our mission. Isaac Kornblatt-Stier provided valuable research assistance, with support from PAFA's archivist Hoang Tran. Judith Thomas, PAFA's director of exhibitions, managed the myriad details of editing, designing, and publishing the volume in partnership with Lucia|Marquand and the University of Pennsylvania Press. Barbara Katus, manager of imaging services, photographed numerous drawings and details within the building. Laurel McLaughlin diligently gathered the many images and permissions. Additional thanks go to L. Jane Calverley, editor, and Susan E. Kelly, designer of this volume.

Thanks also to Melissa Kaiser, executive vice president of development, Marita Blackney, and Zachary Joseph in the development department, and to the Capital Campaign Committee that is helping us to raise the funds necessary to preserve this architectural masterpiece: Kevin F. Donohoe, chairman of the Board of Trustees; Marguerite Lenfest, honorary Campaign chair; Anne E. McCollum and Roger Ballou, Development Committee co-chairs; Donald Caldwell, chairman emeritus; and Jonathan Cohen, Elizabeth Osborne, and Henry DuPont Smith. We are also grateful to Ed Poletti, PAFA's director of facilities management, and Jason Adolff and Roger Chang and the entire design team at DLR Group, who are leading the renovations.

Finally, we would be remiss if we did not thank the photographers past and present who have given us a record of this stunning and ever-evolving building, beginning with Frederick Gutekunst who took the record views in 1876, Harris & Davis who documented the building throughout the 1970s restoration, and, more recently, Lewis Tanner, George Thomas, and Barbara Katus, who are creating the record of the present. From glass negatives to digital files, the building has rewarded the photographers and artists who continue to enliven the galleries.

DAVID R. BRIGHAM
President and CEO
Pennsylvania Academy of the Fine Arts

*William Henry Furness, Inaugural Address, April 22, 1876, Pennsylvania Academy of the Fine Arts, Dorothy and Kenneth Woodcock Archives

Battles on Broad Street—the Academy facade successfully competes with the iconic modern logo and color of a Coca-Cola® truck

Plinth sculpture: KAWS, *BORN TO BEND*, 2014

First Modern

Ahead of the Curve

IN EARLY NOVEMBER 1871, the Pennsylvania Academy of the Fine Arts building committee selected the youthful team of Frank Furness (1839–1912) and George Hewitt (1841–1916) as the winners of an architectural competition to design their new museum and school building. It was a momentous step. For the institution, the resulting building would redefine the Academy. What had been a small museum—where the casts of antique statues on view were utilized as models for art students—would become both a museum of fine arts and a fully functioning school, offering changing exhibitions and training the artists of the nation. In an age when most boards made timid choices that followed historical norms, the Academy building committee belied Philadelphia's reputation for conservative thinking. Instead of selecting a conventional historicizing design, they selected the most original scheme, one that broke with tradition in its logistically based plan, its acceptance of iron and steel systems that brought the power and directness of the modern factory to civic architecture, and in deconstructing historical forms to serve new symbolic purposes. Frank Lloyd Wright's (1857–1959) Solomon R. Guggenheim Museum, New York (fig. 1), and all the star-architect-designed museums ever since, have followed the path chosen by the Academy's adventurous board. Today, there are clear echoes of the Academy across the museum world, from Venturi and Rauch's bold patterning and expressive fenestration at the Allen Memorial Art Museum–Oberlin College, Ohio (fig. 2); to the iconic force of Frank Gehry's (b. 1929) glittering

TOP Pennsylvania Academy of the Fine Arts, attic above the gallery during 1974 restoration BOTTOM Harvard Art Museums skylight, 2011–14. The trusses that carry Renzo Piano's glass roof recall the spidery webs of iron that support the roof above the Academy galleries   11

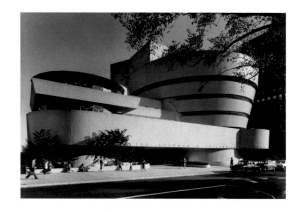

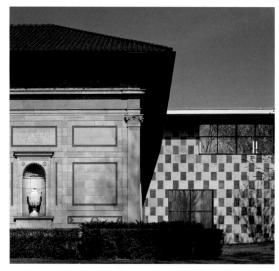

FIG. 1 Frank Lloyd Wright, Guggenheim Museum, New York, 1942, 1953–59. Like Furness's Academy, Wright's museum is composed of distinct forms representing its separate functions

FIG. 2 Venturi and Rauch, Allen Memorial Art Museum–Oberlin College, addition, Oberlin, OH, 1973–76. Strident patterning and functionally placed and sized windows differentiate the new from Cass Gilbert's conventional Beaux-Arts design

FIG. 3 Frank Gehry, Guggenheim Museum, Bilbao, Spain, 1993–97. Computer technologies borrowed from Boeing freed the architect from the tyranny of the I-beam

Guggenheim Museum, Bilbao, Spain (fig. 3); Louis I. Kahn's (1901–1974) top-lighted galleries at the Kimbell Art Museum, Fort Worth, Texas (fig. 4), and Yale University Art Gallery, New Haven, Connecticut; and, most recently, the delicate steel trusses and glass roof above Renzo Piano's (b. 1937) transformed Harvard Art Museums, Cambridge, Massachusetts (pp. 10–11).

The history of modern architecture is usually told through a now-familiar sequence of structures that mark the insertion of industrial technologies into the craft of building and a parallel series of styles that advance and retreat from the possibilities inherent in the new materials. Cast-iron columns appeared in English mills at the end of the eighteenth century, reducing the mass of structure and creating an innovative type of interior space; ever-larger sheets of glass became common in shop fronts in the early nineteenth century, breaking down the boundary between interior and exterior. By 1850, iron and glass were combined in London's Crystal Palace (fig. 8, p. 19), making possible the vast vistas of the hall that housed The Great Exhibition of 1851. From the Crystal Palace to the skyscraper and on to the functional aesthetic of the German Bauhaus, the development of modern architecture required less than seven decades. The Academy warrants a central place in this narrative. Unlike the earlier buildings that made fragmentary and disconnected use of the new industrial materials and systems, the Academy project combined the critical elements of modern logistical planning, steel and iron construction, and modern plumbing, heating, and ventilation systems, serving as a workplace and a school, with the architectural expression of the age. Moreover, rather than seeking to reify the past, the architects had chosen the most dynamic of modern forces—the machine—as both inspiration and ornament. Instead of being based on a look into the rearview mirror of history, the new Academy faced the present and the future. This created a civic museum and school building whose expressive style referenced both its updated purpose and a novel attitude toward the past. The Academy's machine for making art can rightly be termed the first modern building.[1]

*   *   *

FIG. 4 Louis I. Kahn, Kimbell Art Museum, Fort Worth, TX, 1967–72. Top-lighted galleries with light diffusers that change with exterior conditions, recalling the dynamic lighting of the Academy

FURNESS & HEWITT

Frank Furness and George Wattson Hewitt were both born in Philadelphia, but, within a few years, their lives diverged in directions that marked their future careers. Furness would grow up in the heart of the burgeoning industrial city, amidst a heady circle of intellectual exploration guided by his father, the Reverend Dr. William Henry Furness (1802–1896; fig. 5), who led the city's First Unitarian congregation. Dr. Furness brought from Boston his Harvard training and his life-long friendship with Ralph Waldo Emerson (1803–1882; fig. 6, p. 16), whose writings and American-centered philosophy would shape young Frank's perspective. Emerson's perceptions would be spread as American scriptures for designers through Furness's students, Louis Sullivan (1856–1924) and William L. Price (1861–1916), and via Sullivan to Frank Lloyd Wright.

The Hewitt family, by contrast, moved from the booming industrial city to Burlington, New Jersey, a peaceful village on the Delaware River, where the father taught music. George attended the local preparatory school, Burlington College, founded by the Episcopal community with the goal of maintaining traditional values in a rapidly changing world. In 1857, Hewitt's schooling ended and he entered the Philadelphia office of builder/engineer/architect Joseph Hoxie (1804–1870). There he encountered the modern scale and engineering demands of railroad design, overlaid with Hoxie's conservative architectural modeling. He soon left for the office of Scots-born architect John Notman (1810–1865), the principal designer of elite Episcopal churches in the Philadelphia region.

Furness, after apprenticing locally with the politically connected John Fraser (1825–1906), was sent to New York in 1857 to study with École des Beaux-Arts-trained Richard Morris Hunt (1827–1895) in Hunt's atelier in the Studio Building on 10th Street. There he joined a cluster of Harvard alumni, including Henry Van Brunt (1832–1903), William Ware (1832–1915), Charles D. Gambrill (1832–1880; later a partner of Henry Hobson Richardson, 1838–1886), and New York University graduate George B. Post (1837–1913), all

TOP Frederick Gutekunst, portrait of Frank Furness, c. 1873

BOTTOM George Wattson Hewitt, c. 1885

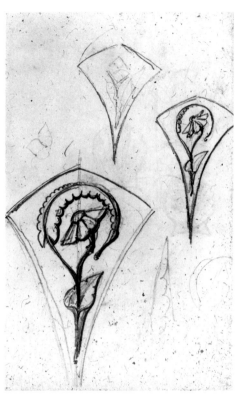

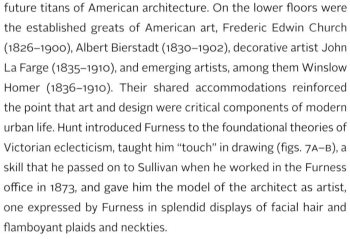

future titans of American architecture. On the lower floors were the established greats of American art, Frederic Edwin Church (1826–1900), Albert Bierstadt (1830–1902), decorative artist John La Farge (1835–1910), and emerging artists, among them Winslow Homer (1836–1910). Their shared accommodations reinforced the point that art and design were critical components of modern urban life. Hunt introduced Furness to the foundational theories of Victorian eclecticism, taught him "touch" in drawing (figs. 7A–B), a skill that he passed on to Sullivan when he worked in the Furness office in 1873, and gave him the model of the architect as artist, one expressed by Furness in splendid displays of facial hair and flamboyant plaids and neckties.

The young men's paths diverged again in 1861. Hewitt joined the 52nd Regiment of the Pennsylvania Volunteers on a three-month enlistment and then quickly returned to architectural work with Notman. Furness, loyal to his father's abolitionist cause, enlisted for three years with the 6th Pennsylvania Cavalry, a much-decorated regiment that saw extensive duty through Gettysburg and the Virginia campaign; one particularly heroic act of carrying ammunition to an exposed outpost across the field of battle would later result in his being awarded the Congressional Medal of Honor. In 1864, he returned to New York and Hunt's office. When he received a commission for a Unitarian Church in the Germantown section of

FIG. 5 John Sartain (1808–1897) after William Henry Furness Jr. (1828–1867), *Reverend William Henry Furness*, 1862–65. Mezzotint, etching, engraving and stipple on off-white wove paper, Pennsylvania Academy of the Fine Arts

FIGS. 7A–B Frank Furness, pencil in notebook, c. 1875, "touch" drawing showing the evolution of a flower ornament above the Academy's school entrance and realized decoration on the Cherry Street facade (detail)

Philadelphia, Furness married and began his Philadelphia practice. He was soon recruited by his erstwhile teacher, Fraser, who doubtless saw the advantage of hiring a connected young war hero; a year later, in 1867, after the death of Notman, they added George Hewitt to their masthead, creating the firm of Fraser, Furness & Hewitt.

The dimensions of the practice reflected their experiences and their connections. Fraser had designed the city's Union League headquarters on Broad Street, a massive brownstone and red brick Second Empire–styled building, and had a politically connected practice of Philadelphia school buildings and Presbyterian churches. Furness brought the most up-to-date knowledge of design practice and an array of clients, many of whom reflected his father's religious connections—including the Jewish community, for whom the firm would design Rodef Shalom Synagogue and the Jewish Hospital—as well as entrée into the intellectual circles of the city. Hewitt brought his connections to the Episcopal community, leading to numerous church commissions as well as houses for members of those churches.

Instead of functioning like a smoothly running troika, the office pulled in three directions at once: Fraser looking backward to pre–Civil War designs and public projects; Hewitt essaying the English; and Furness beginning the exploration of architectural identity and contemporary technologies that would mark his later career. In 1871, when the Pennsylvania Academy of the Fine Arts competition was announced, Furness and Hewitt entered the Academy competition without Fraser, effectively breaking up their partnership. The revised office settled into the partitioned practice recalled by Sullivan. Once again the dynamics were unstable, and in 1875, even before the completion of the Academy building, Hewitt and Furness went their separate ways.

Their future practices continued along the paths that their lives had determined. Hewitt, working with his brother William (1847–1924) in the firm of G. W. & W. D. Hewitt, found remarkable success looking to historical sources, a direction that coincided with the rise of corporate, "Gilded Age" America. Among his hundreds of projects were Philadelphia's Bourse and Bellevue Stratford Hotel, dozens of remarkable historically derived mansions for corporate leaders, and projects that spanned the nation, from George Boldt's castle on the St. Lawrence River to a hotel in Tacoma, Washington.

Furness and various successor firms, beginning with Allen Evans (1849–1925) in Furness & Evans, and later Furness, Evans & Co., found their clients in the industrial culture of the city, absorbed the lessons of its progressive machinery engineers, and designed nearly eight hundred projects that gave Philadelphia its architectural identity, one that persisted into the late twentieth century in the architecture of Louis I. Kahn and Venturi, Scott Brown and Associates. Where his peers focused on the traditions of architectural design, Furness and his students looked forward, changing the course of American and global design and representing the moment when Philadelphia—led by a culture shaped by the applied sciences and industry—made the present and the future the focus of their buildings.

*　　*　　*

FIG. 6　William Henry Furness Jr. (1828–1867), *Ralph Waldo Emerson*, c. 1867. Oil on canvas, unfinished, Pennsylvania Academy of the Fine Arts

FIG. 8 Joseph Paxton, Crystal Palace exhibition hall, London, 1851 (destroyed). In its lightness of material and economy of construction, the Crystal Palace was recognized as a superb model for exhibition pavilions, influencing later structures such as those for the Philadelphia Centennial Exhibition

Cause and Effect

ACROSS THE MODERN WORLD, buildings have been influenced, sometimes directly, sometimes indirectly, by the possibilities made visible in the Pennsylvania Academy of the Fine Arts. Unlike its more traditional ecclesiastical, civic, and commercial neighbors that line North Broad Street, the Academy's massing and its carefully placed and sized windows begin a conversation with the viewer about the variety of functions within—entrance, administrative offices, gallery, school, and studios—each of which is expressed on the boldly colored exterior. In the Philadelphia of 1871, which

was soon to host the American Centennial Exhibition, the United States' second world's fair, the original manner had a purpose: allying the Academy with the progressive industrial future that rivaled the political revolution of 1776 as the true focus of the fair and the city. When it was completed in time for the 1876 Centennial, the Academy, like the Crystal Palace a generation earlier (fig. 8), made a revolutionary statement about the power of the industrial culture and the mechanical forces that were shaping Philadelphia and its institutions. Both transcended their era—but the Academy continues as a vital working building in the modern world.

On every surface, exterior and interior, machine-based iconography pervades the Academy fabric. The ornamental passages of its public facades have a crisp sharpness made possible by a newly invented industrial technique that, instead of relying on hand-craft, blasted the details into being with jets of sand through a rubber pattern (see p. 45).[2] Details derived from modern machines—control knobs, ball-bearing rings, pistons, and drive shafts—ornament the

Joseph M. Wilson, Machinery Hall, Philadelphia Centennial Grounds, 1875–76 (demolished)

TOP Wilson's use of off-the-shelf materials and industrial elements followed the model of industrial age economy in the exterior of the Machinery Hall

BOTTOM The interior of the Machinery Hall was more frankly industrial with light trusses stabilizing the structure and standardized parts and ceiling heights, determined, along with the length of the hall, by the optimum runs for the drive shafts that powered machines and rotated the wheels of giant locomotives

FIG. 9 The lamps at the Academy's Broad Street entrance are accented with devices borrowed from contemporary machine control knobs, ball-bearing-like rings, and piston-like shafts   FIG. 10 Unlike the usual grandiose Victorian stair with turned balusters, the Academy's railing incorporates abstracted versions of the drive shafts and universal joints that powered the machines of the region's great factories

bronze lamps at the entrance (fig. 9) and the railings of the main stair (fig. 10), continuing in the piston-like columns of the galleries. These details pale before the immense iron truss (figs. 11B and 15) that occupies much of the north facade along Cherry Street (now Lenfest Plaza). It carries the gallery walls of the upper story, while making possible a continuous band of skylights that provided even north-facing light for the studios of the school on the first floor. Here, instead of load-bearing arches that would have blocked light from the studios, defeating the purpose of the skylight, the architects made use of a system straight out of regional industry. Rather than concealing this remarkable feature behind classically detailed panels or bands of Gothic ornament, the architects acknowledged its potency by exposing the bridge-like structure for its entire length, highlighting it for emphasis by paralleling its

diagonals with decorative brickwork between the iron struts. The strip window of the skylight became a motif of the Bauhaus, while more recent architects have brought the structural truss to the surface—as in Skidmore, Owings & Merrill's Hancock Center in Chicago, Norman Foster's (b. 1935) Hearst Building in New York City (fig. 12), Renzo Piano, Richard Rogers (b. 1933) and Gianfranco Franchini's (1938–2009) Pompidou Centre in Paris (fig. 13), and, most recently, Rem Koolhaas's (b. 1944) Seattle Public Library, with its upper "living room" spanned by giant trusses that are visible through the exterior glass skin at night (fig. 14).

The Academy, however, was more than a tour de force of the coming structural innovations that would lead to tall buildings and vast interior column-free spaces; it was also a visual compendium of historical and global styles drawn from chronologically distant

FIGS. 11A–B Frederick Gutekunst, Pennsylvania Academy of the Fine Arts, 1876 (details)

LEFT The Broad Street facade was conceived as a billboard for art, with a fourth-century-BCE Greek sculpture above the main entrance and stacked elements of a Grecian Doric frieze, sculpted metope panels, and grooved triglyphs panels on a field of Ruskinian Gothic color and detail   RIGHT The right side of the photo displays the industrial roots with factory roof ventilators, the loft-like gallery carried on a giant steel truss, and the glass roof lighting the studios

worlds. There were echoes of ancient Greece and the Middle Ages, drawn from sources as far away as the modern Middle East and Mogul India and as near as the muscular, but relatively mute, industrial buildings of Philadelphia. When the Academy was being designed, architects typically adopted historical styles more or less in their entirety, rather than concocting eclectic pastiches. Styles were selected to express function and cultural associations, such as Florentine bankers' palazzi for banks and commerce, medieval fortresses for prisons, ecclesiastical variations of Gothic for churches, and so on. Instead of restricting their choices to one

mode, Furness & Hewitt mixed familiar motifs from the presumably incompatible opposites of classical and Gothic styles (fig. 11A). They broke apart and reconstituted standard features, such as the linear, repeating pattern of triglyphs and metopes of the Grecian Doric frieze, to create a stacked system of parts, one above the other. They piled massive industrial ventilating monitors from factory architecture atop French mansard roofs and juxtaposed an authentic fourth-century-BCE Greek sculpture—which they placed on the plinth above the main entrance—with modern sculpted representations of a contemporary painting in the great hall of the

CLOCKWISE FROM TOP

FIG. 12 Foster & Partners, Hearst Tower, New York, 2006. The diagonal bracing of the steel frame is expressed in the shape of the tower

FIG. 13 Richard Rogers, Renzo Piano, Gianfranco Franchini, Arup Partners, Pompidou Centre, Paris, France, 1971–77. A celebration of the systems and materials of modern construction, the Centre uses color to represent various functions

FIG. 14 Rem Koolhaas, Office of Metropolitan Architecture, Seattle Public Library, 1999–2004. The structural trusses that carry the building are visible at night through the diaphanous glass skin

French national design school, the École des Beaux-Arts. And to the horror of fellow architects and critics alike, they inserted a structurally unnecessary pier under the center of the main entry arch, a motif that was carried inside to the opening into the monumental stair. The architects then selected a variety of materials that made a flag-like surface of colors and strident patterns along the Broad Street and Cherry Street facades (figs. 16–17). Purplish brownstone, cherry-red and coal-black bricks, pale yellow sandstone, stained and enameled glass—and the aforementioned iron truss, painted lead-oxide red—were manhandled into patterns that anticipated late-twentieth-century post-modernism's abstraction, fracturing, and anti-contextual use of historic styles. The result was an eye-catching billboard, a mashup of details from the conventional fine arts palace merged with the rigor, logic, and singleness of purpose of a factory. When it was built, there was nothing like it in the world.

The architectural license of the exterior continued unabated into the interior, where the designers again broke new ground. Instead of adapting a plan from an existing church or school, the arrangement of spaces in the Academy was based on the straightforward acceptance of the logistics of its uses. The entrance sequence for the public begins with the lobby, which leads directly to the over-scaled main stair that visually blocks access to the private school spaces at the rear of the building and then passes through a loft-like volume containing galleries above and school below. It ends at the rear with a gigantic elevator designed to lift

FIG. 15 Instead of concealing the steel truss, the architects celebrated it as a principal element of the Cherry Street facade, reinforcing its design with patterned brickwork

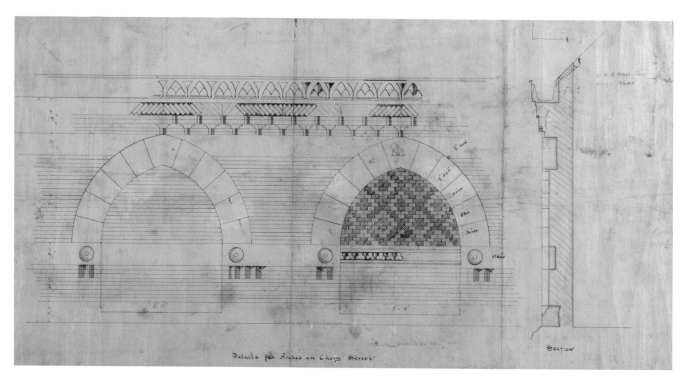

Details for Arches on Cherry Street

Section

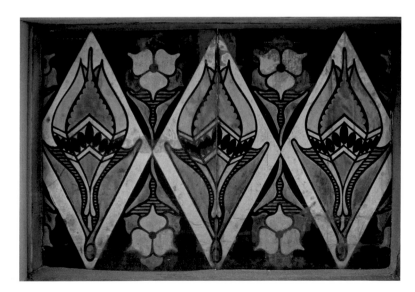

OPPOSITE

FIG. 16 Furness & Hewitt, *Details of arches on Cherry Street facade*, c. 1872. The carefully detailed elevation drawing of the lower arcade would have been among the earliest drawings

FIG. 17 The resulting cherry-red and coal-black brickwork is accented with pale-yellow sandstone above the hammered purplish brownstone foundation

RIGHT FIGS. 18A–C Stained and enameled glass panels, backed with gold foil, accent the upper levels of the Broad Street facade that Furness described as like "the iridescence of a beetle's wing"

animals to the studio level for painting and drawing classes and the large artworks of the Gilded Age to the gallery level. On the first floor, muscular riveted plate girders (fig. 19) span the auditorium; on the main gallery level, divisions in the largest room and between the central long corridor and the crossing are carried by wrought-iron U-channels (fig. 20), bolted together and supported on columns made of iron pipes. Gallery ceilings are spanned with metal grids hung on iron rods from the steel structure overhead carrying glass plates. The surrounding perimeter iron frames of the skylights are pierced with decorative shapes to allow the flow of air into the attic (p. 27). The skylights bring glowing but modulated light into every nook and cranny of the gallery level and into the teaching spaces of the lower school studios. Instead of the customary static experience of an artificially lit gallery, the Academy's spaces change with the seasons, the time of day, and even with the passage of a cloud, making every visit a different experience. At the top of the building, above the skylights and invisible to most visitors, is a zone of unadorned industrial construction. The workhorses of this space are rough brick piers forming an arcade running the length of the building, with the exception of the zone interrupted by the cross gallery, which is spanned by giant steel trusses (figs. 21A–B). A factory-like ventilating roof monitor runs the length of the main block to cool the building by

FIG. 19 Cast-iron columns and riveted-steel girders, spanning the auditorium, brought industrial materials into a civic space

FIG. 20 Inexpensive rolled-steel pipes serve as columns and carry riveted wrought-iron U-channels to span spaces in the auditorium, the rotunda gallery, and the largest of the public galleries

OPPOSITE Despite the familiar Gothic-revival capitals and arches, the materials of the great hall reflect the new industrial age in piston-like stone columns, pulley-gear-like ornamental forms, and pierced cast-iron skylight frames to permit air flow from the gallery into the attic and out of the roof ventilators

means of banks of operable louvers (fig. 22) joined by steel rods and operated by pulleys from the gallery level (fig. 23). Finally, the roofs above the galleries are sheathed in glass plates supported on spidery webs of iron (fig. 24A), attenuated so as not to cast shadows on the art below.

In its directness, its expression of purpose, its adaptation of new means to specific ends, and in its additive character, the Academy has the circumstantial appearance of the great machines (fig. 25) being created in Philadelphia during the same period. These machines were complicated affairs of steam boilers, pistons, flywheels, and regulators, with each assembly serving and expressing a particular function, the basis of modern steampunk rather than the streamlined packages of the 1930s or the minimalist perfection of the Apple products of today. As engineers added new protective

FIGS. 21 A–B The large span of the rotunda gallery required a gap in the masonry arcade that is bridged by steel trusses like those on the Cherry Street facade

FIG. 22 Interior temperature was controlled by a factory-like roof monitor that runs the length of the gallery

FIG. 23 The ventilating monitor carries a bank of operable louvers, ganged together with steel rods in a standard factory system that could be operated from the gallery level

FIGS. 24A–B   LEFT The roofs above the side galleries are supported on minimal trusses held in compression by tie rods that minimize shadows on the art below RIGHT Nearly a century and a half later, Renzo Piano used similar systems for the new roof of the Harvard Art Museums

OPPOSITE, CLOCKWISE FROM BOTTOM

FIG. 25 Baldwin Locomotive, from Joseph M. Wilson, *The Masterpieces of the Centennial International Exhibition,* 3 (Philadelphia: Gebbie & Barrie, 1876)

FIG. 26 A motif derived from the counterweights of locomotive wheels ornaments the iron gates at the student entrance

FIG. 27 The lamps of the main staircase continued the mechanical detailing with spring-like bases and punched ornaments

devices, governors, pressure valves, and counterweights, they created an alternate design strategy to the reductive classical or the ascetic Gothic styles, one that worked with engineers' logic from means to ends. In this additive system, refinements expressed specific improvements, but they rarely simplified.

Critics examining detail and historians researching in archives have yet to connect the Academy's new building to the machine culture and the underlying machine metaphors that enabled Frank Furness to chart a path out of the maze of Victorian cultural confusion toward the freedom of modern architecture. Furness's engagement with the machine culture that was transforming Philadelphia is everywhere apparent in the details of the Academy building (figs. 26–27), although it takes eyes attuned to nineteenth-century forms to recognize their meaning. Few today recognize the decorative forms at the base of the iron gates of

FIG. 28 Louis I. Kahn, Richards Medical Research Laboratories, University of Pennsylvania, Philadelphia, 1957–60, 1962. Forms express purpose with towers containing circulation and ventilation, while cantilevered glazed corners house the work spaces

FIG. 29 Venturi and Rauch, Dixwell Fire Station, New Haven, CT, 1967. Fenestration and volumes denote the usual features of a fire house, from the central hose drying tower to the giant garage portal

the front and rear entrances as derived from the counterweights of locomotive wheels; they are equally unaware that the universal joints and drive shafts of factory power systems are referenced in the bronze stair railings, and most overlook the ball-bearing-like ornamental bands and piston-like shafts of the lamps of the main facade. Without an understanding of nineteenth-century machines, Furness's details seem arbitrary, but viewed through the lens of his sources, the machine and the new materials of the industrial age, his architecture becomes explicable. These sources would inform Furness's work to the end of his career.

Despite the assaults on convention, tradition, and the standard practices of their day mounted by Furness & Hewitt, to our twenty-first-century eyes the Academy reads as a creation of the Victorian moment in its visual complexity, its piling up of stylistic motifs, and its solid mass and relatively low bulk. It is obviously not a mid-twentieth-century Miesian classical modern building of related elements refined to sleek, planar perfection. Nor is it a late-twentieth-century Frank Gehry–designed, shape-shifting, reflective-surfaced, computer-technology-based form. Instead, the new museum and school are an antecedent to another more descriptive modern mode that leads to late Le Corbusier (1887–1965), Louis I. Kahn (fig. 28), Robert Venturi (b. 1925; fig. 29), and even to Rem Koolhaas. Like their designs, the Academy is a factual celebration of particularity, amplified beyond mere utility to assert its role as a work of art (fig. 30). But unlike modern buildings that are constructed of materials that are made by machines and trend toward largeness of scale and simplicity of surface, Furness & Hewitt's first masterpiece contrasts a fineness of detail and a Victorian sensibility of small-scale materials. These are made to fit the hand, alongside giant modern elements such as the steel truss and the strip skylight of the Cherry Street facade, and the immense stone panels of the Broad Street front. Much of the Academy's energy comes from these deliberate juxtapositions.

*　　*　　*

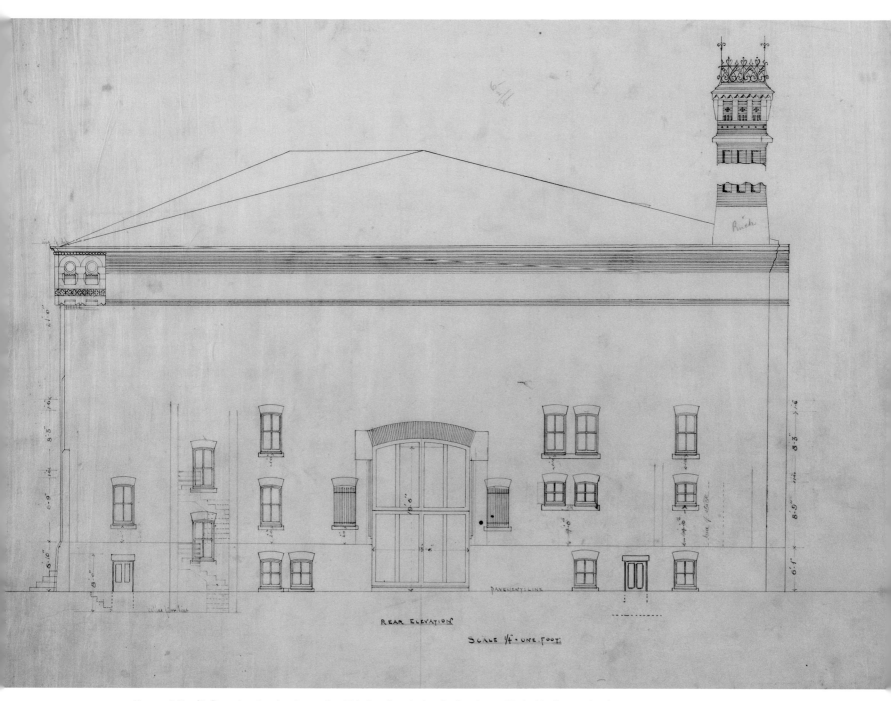

REAR ELEVATION

SCALE 1/4 = ONE FOOT

FIG. 30 Furness & Hewitt, *Rear elevation drawing*, c. 1872. This describes the interior functions, with the big elevator door in the center, stepped windows indicating a stair, and other windows denoting the porter's quarters

FIG. 31 John Dorsey (1759–1821), Pennsylvania Academy of the Fine Arts, 1805–06 (demolished), engraving by Cephas G. Childs (1793–1871) after George Strickland (1791–1851)

ART FROM TRADITION TO INNOVATION

The changing nature of the Academy's collections offers one explanation for the transformation of nineteenth-century architecture. When it was founded in 1805, the Academy was an artistic and aesthetic outpost of the representational tradition, rooted in the British school of artists led by Joshua Reynolds (1723–1792) and his American expatriate colleague, Benjamin West (1738–1820). Their methods and subjects are apt parallels to the first Academy buildings, which were part of the long British tradition of Greco-Roman classicism (fig. 31). Like these buildings, the paintings of the British school drew on historical themes; some depicted virtuous heroism, others were a sort of reportage art, showing aspects of the new scientific knowledge of the Enlightenment. These were augmented by the mainstay of the artist, portraits of individuals whose identities were enhanced by standard attributes: urns for family

history, uniforms and swords for military prowess and allegiance, children for the future. The human figure was learned from classical sculptures, not from the live model or from anatomy, infusing the postures of their subjects with gestures, stances, proportions, and expressions from the distant past. A notable subgroup of British artists depicted topographically identifiable landscapes that connoted the surviving feudal power of land ownership. Despite their variation in subject matter, all of these paintings were set in constructed spaces that recede from the picture plane.

By the middle of the nineteenth century, the arts were in a wild state of flux as the late-seventeenth-century aesthetic battle between the "Ancients and the Moderns" was supplanted first by the rationalism of the Enlightenment and then the rising personalization and sentiment of the romantic Victorians; by the

John Neagle (1796–1865), *Pat Lyon at the Forge* (detail), 1829.
Oil on canvas, Pennsylvania Academy of the Fine Arts

FIG. 32 Thomas Eakins (1844–1916), *Cowboy: Study for Cowboys in Badlands*, c. 1887–88. Oil on canvas on panel, Denver Museum of Art

mid-nineteenth century, the focus was on images of everyday life that presaged what critic Arthur Danto (1924–2013) labels "The Transfiguration of the Commonplace." The broad narratives of art history have too often been told from the internal perspective of aesthetics, as a sequence of styles playing off one another; but as a part of life, art, like architecture, demands a broader cultural frame that situates its subjects and methods in its time and place. Those cultural shifts are evident in the canvases of America's artists even before the Civil War (1861–1865), when they caught the rising tide of an affluent and ever-larger middle class and painted subjects that were not dependent on prior knowledge from a classical education. John Neagle's (1798–1865) early-nineteenth-century portrait *Pat Lyon at the Forge* (1829; see p. 34) put the viewer in the craftsman's shop, albeit one rendered allegorically; the Philadelphia jail where Lyon had been imprisoned is viewed through a window and the Pythagorean Theorem is demonstrated on a sheet of paper in the foreground as a means of attesting to Lyon's rectitude after he had been accused of theft. Subsequent to the Civil War, Thomas Eakins's (1844–1916) brilliantly lit scenes of rowing on the Schuylkill or his quickly brushed sketches of cowboys in the American West (c. 1887–88; fig. 32) gained a

journalistic freshness and a scientific exactitude not unlike those of his New England counterpart, Winslow Homer. The viewer is placed in the moment by Homer, within rather than outside of an experience, in works such as his watercolors of a trout grabbing a fly, drawn from the perspective of the fish; or his oil painting of a fox in deep snow being harassed by crows (1893; fig. 33), viewed from above in a bird's-eye view; or the brilliance of light in his depiction of an endless Bahamian summer. Though both Eakins and Homer were trained in the methods of glazes and overlays that linked their art to the visual reserve of the classical tradition, by the early 1870s their canvases were shifting toward the contemporary subjects, dynamic compositions, and visual immediacy that could be read in depth or across the picture plane, leading to the continuous revolutions that characterize modern art.

The new art, both in subject and style, was part of a vast nineteenth-century cultural watershed, as industrialization, urbanization, and ever-increasing tides of secularization remade every aspect of work and life. Daily routine was ruled by the clock rather than the sun. Ever-more sophisticated sciences, using the microscope and the laboratory, disproved and then supplanted the old cultural truths based in the Bible and the classics of ancient Greece and Rome.[3] Instead of accepting handed-down conventions, scientists sought new knowledge gained from intense observation, systematic experimentation, and record keeping that proved or disproved the validity of theories. In turn, this ultimately forced the reevaluation and rejection of most of what had passed for higher learning. The developing knowledge ended the idea of authority centered in tradition and history, emblemized in architecture by the orders and then the styles, and, as in Henry James's (1843–1916) *Madonna of the Future* (1867), achieved by copying and recopying ancient masters. In their place came new possibilities, drawing from the active forces of modern life and creating new ways of visualization, and taller buildings made possible by new structural materials that linked design to the dynamic processes inherent in modernity.

*   *   *

FIG. 33 Winslow Homer (1836–1910), *Fox Hunt*, 1893. Oil on canvas, Pennsylvania Academy of the Fine Arts

FIG. 34 Charles Willson Peale (1741–1827), *Exhumation of the Mastodon*, 1806–8. Oil on canvas, Maryland Historical Society

PEALE'S MUSEUM

Half a century before the 1871 competition for the present Academy building, Charles Willson Peale (1741–1827) had painted *The Artist in His Museum* (1822), hinting at the coming turmoil of the age.[4] The artist portrayed himself as a relic from the days of the American Revolution, in the frock coat, knee breeches, and stockings of eighteenth-century fashion. He stands in front of a vast room containing portraits of his fellow revolutionaries and his collection of American natural history arranged in Linnaean order. At his feet are several of the wonders of the nascent nation: the carcass of a wild turkey, by then nearly hunted to extinction, and, most remarkable, the giant leg bones and jawbone of the creature screened behind the curtain that Peale lifts with his right hand, making him a modern commercial figure, a showman, like the later P. T. Barnum. The skeleton was that of a mastodon, the pre-historic elephant-like creature whose excavation Peale had led in 1800 and which he had memorialized in his monumental painting, *Exhumation of the Mastodon* (1806–8; fig. 34).[5]

Fossilized bones of prehistoric creatures were but one of many physical discoveries that undermined the credibility of the Bible and the texts of the ancient philosophers as a reliable source for science and history. In turn, these remains stimulated Charles Darwin's (1809–1882) theory, published as *The Origin of Species* (1859), which demonstrated that modern species were not handed directly from God, but instead were shaped by natural selection in response to their environment. Darwin's scheme of systematic progression to meet changing realities could be tied to any type of human endeavor, including architecture. The world was everywhere in flux, and the artists that we now remember were quick to capture the new age in the drama of a surgical procedure, the energy of modern city street life, or the pastoral charm of a day in the park—all of these views enlivened by young people in fashionable garb.

*   *   *

Charles Willson Peale (1741–1827), *The Artist in His Museum* (detail), 1822.
Oil on canvas, Pennsylvania Academy of the Fine Arts

Architecture in the City of Applied Science

GREAT ARCHITECTURE ENGAGES WITH and expresses the circumstances and opportunities of its creation. For much of the nineteenth and twentieth centuries, Philadelphia has been caricatured as controlled by Quakers, whose seventeenth-century rejection of ornament and decoration—to place the focus on the person and not their wealth—caused them to be viewed as indifferent, even hostile, to aesthetics. This led outsiders to explain the daring and unconventional works of Frank Furness as an expression of Quaker antagonism to the arts, as when the critic for the Boston-based *American Architect and Building News* reviewed Philadelphia design at the end of the Centennial year and concluded that, in Quaker Philadelphia, the arts, like a defective newborn child, were "quietly smothered."[6] In fact, Philadelphia Quakers had largely divorced themselves from cultural leadership of their city during the second half of the eighteenth century and the first half of the nineteenth century, making it necessary to find alternative explanations for the Academy design. Better explanations were always hiding in plain sight.

Forty-two years before the design competition for the Academy, Scottish essayist Thomas Carlyle (1795–1881) had proclaimed the arrival of a "mechanical age" that would undo many of the traditional conventions and practices of pre-industrial culture, substituting the amorality of mechanics and the sciences for the cultural morality embedded in history.[7] As an example of the new age, Carlyle offered the Lancasterian school building[8] with its twelve classrooms, one for each grade, in which students advanced year by year, so that school buildings became, in his phrase, "machines for Education." Furness & Hewitt's Pennsylvania Academy of the Fine Arts, with its highly specific studios (fig. 37, p. 43), classrooms, library, and gallery, was a machine in a similar way—not by extruding students through a linear and cumulative educational process, but by providing tightly conceived settings to serve particular activities. Anticipating Le Corbusier's description of a house as "a machine for living," the Academy was a machine for making and viewing art, in every way aimed at the future, rather than the traditional past.

The gargantuan scale of Philadelphia industry is evident in this interior view of the Baldwin Locomotive Works, a few blocks north of the Academy building, where giant overhead cranes carried entire locomotives, c. 1893

FIG. 35 The Baldwin Locomotive Works, from J. Thomas Scharf and Thompson Westcott, *History of Philadelphia: 1609–1884*, 3 (Philadelphia: L. H. Everts, 1884). The works occupied nearly a dozen city blocks, interspersed with other manufacturers of railroad wheels and machine tools, positioning this district as the center of innovation in the industrial age

FIG. 36 Workers' row houses, 24th and Kimball Streets, Philadelphia, 1916. Factory districts contained thousands of two-story houses, whose every material, from the bricks and cut-stone trim to the pressed-metal cornices and door and window assemblies, was mass produced

The new building was appropriate to its city because, at the end of the Civil War, Philadelphia was the American city that had been most transformed by industrialization. This status was embodied in the city's core cultural institution, the Franklin Institute of the State of Pennsylvania for the Promotion of the Mechanical Arts. Founded in 1824, the Institute became a magnet that drew creative

mechanics, industrialists, and inventors from around the nation and the world to Philadelphia and its industries. With its array of classes in the sciences and applied fields from mechanical drawing to architecture, its lectures, conferences, competitions, and prizes, the Institute would become America's premier applied-science organization, retaining that status until colleges and universities took over the combined teaching and research roles at the end of the nineteenth century. From a cultural perspective, it epitomized Philadelphia in the way that athenaeums denoted New England cities, representing the underlying values and aspirations that set the directions of their communities. Where athenaeums, by their name, proclaimed allegiance to classical learning and traditional cultural forms, the Franklin Institute focused Philadelphia's conversation on the sciences, engineering, and issues of contemporary life that had interested its namesake, Benjamin Franklin (1706–1790). And unlike New England athenaeums and regional groups such as the Historical Society of Pennsylvania (first meeting, October 9, 1824), whose membership was limited by invitation and the backward-looking focus of the organization, the Institute meetings were open to all, bringing together educated professors, imaginative engineers, driven industrialists, and practical workmen to share discussion in the same space.[9] As the Civil War ended, the Institute had become the primary agent of Philadelphia's control of American industry, establishing the systems and the methods of industrial standardization, and later, scientific management.[10]

In 1867, the Franklin Institute's board proposed to sponsor an international exhibition to celebrate the nation's Centennial in the city where the Declaration of Independence had been written. But, to further their business interests, it was proposed that the main focus of the exhibition should not be on past glories, but on the great machines being manufactured in Philadelphia, and the new age that they augured. Centennial-era Philadelphia was a global center of applied science innovation. The nation's largest transportation business, the Pennsylvania Railroad, was headquartered in the city and applied the Institute's doctrine of industrial standardization to all of its suppliers. Philadelphia's largest employer, the Baldwin Locomotive Works (fig. 35), was located along with innovative machine tool designers and manufacturers north of Vine Street, in the nineteenth-century steam-powered equivalent of today's Silicon Valley. Giant factories provided the rising wages

FIG. 37 The structural systems that underlie the light-filled spaces of the Academy are particularly visible in the studios. Giant bolts mark the underside of the truss carrying the gallery above the skylights of the cast studio, with the steel beams and brick vaults of the fire-proof floors also visible

that turned Philadelphia workers into consumers; blocks of mass-produced workers' row houses (fig. 36) extended in all directions; eventually a dozen department stores, serving all the subgroups of the city's populace, lined Market Street, each providing evidence of the positive impact of the industrial economy on everyday life.

By mid-century, torrents of new industrial wealth brought civic-minded inventors and engineers to the boards of institutions such as the American Academy of Music and the University of Pennsylvania, and, in 1852, to the board of the Pennsylvania Academy of the Fine Arts with the elevation of industrialist Matthias Baldwin

(1795–1866). As engineers and inventors conveyed their values to their boards, they began to shape institutions in ways that were astonishing to those from other cities that had not accepted the industrial culture and its progressive values, and remained tied to the old historical sources and narratives. It would be these creative men and their progressive strategies, rooted in the modern machines and industrial systems that they were inventing, who would become Furness's clients.

*   *   *

FIRST BOARD AND
THE BOARD FOR THE 1871 BUILDING

The Academy's first board, seated in 1805, represented the forces of a mercantile city. The inaugural president, George Clymer (1739–1813), was a member of the Religious Society of Friends, a merchant, a member of the Continental Congress, a signer of the Declaration of Independence, and an indispensable institutional leader who managed many of the boards of the city.[11] The other members were William Tilghman (1756–1827), lawyer and chief justice of the Pennsylvania State Supreme Court; William Rawle (1759–1836), Quaker lawyer and boardman at the University of Pennsylvania, the Library Company of Philadelphia, and a founder of the Historical Society of Pennsylvania; Moses Levy (1757–1826), lawyer, presiding judge and recorder of Philadelphia; Joseph Hopkinson (1770–1842), lawyer, boardman, and US congressman; Joseph B. McKean (1764–1826), lawyer, judge, and Pennsylvania state attorney general; William Meredith (1772–1844), lawyer, boardman, and banker; William Rush (1756–1833), sculptor and instructor at the Academy; John R. Coxe (1773–1864), medical doctor, boardman, and later professor of medicine; John Dorsey (c. 1759–1821), merchant, amateur architect, and boardman; William Poyntell (1756–1811), British-born merchant and early art collector; Thomas C. James (1766–1835), medical doctor, secretary of the American Philosophical Society, and afterwards president of the College of Physicians; and Charles Willson Peale (1741–1827), artist, naturalist, soldier, and founder of the earlier short-lived organization devoted to the arts, the Columbiana. Clymer's successor as president was Hopkinson, who also served on the board of the University of Pennsylvania. Among his side interests was poetry; he wrote the words to "Hail Columbia," which for most of the nineteenth century was the national anthem.

The 1870 board represented the new industrial culture, albeit with a few survivors from the earlier board: president Caleb Cope (1797–1888), banker and silk merchant; and members George S. Pepper (1808–1890), philanthropist and boardman; John Bohlen (1815–1874), gentleman, donor, and art collector; A. May Stevenson (1806–1888), merchant and art collector; and James L. Claghorn (1817–1884), auctioneer and financier. The remainder were part of the new culture: William Struthers (1812–1876), stone yard owner and member of the Franklin Institute (hereafter MFI); Alfred D. Jessup (1826–1881), paper manufacturer, industrialist, and MFI; Henry C. Gibson (1830–1891), liquor distiller and art collector; Joseph Harrison Jr. (1810–1874), engineer, steam engine manufacturer, and MFI; J. Gillingham Fell (1816–1878), civil engineer, coal and railroad industrialist, donor, and MFI; John Sartain (1808–1897), artist, engraver, and MFI; Dr. F[rancis]. W. Lewis (1826–1902), medical doctor, founder of Children's Hospital, and an art collector; and Henry G. Morris (1839–1915), engineer, iron manufacturer, and MFI.

*   *   *

Most of the ornament of the Academy is the work of modern technology: the decorative plaster pieces of the walls are cast; the stone columns were turned on steam-powered lathes; the pattern of the stone panels was sandblasted through a rubber stencil

The Changing Board: Businessmen, Manufacturing Interests, and a "New Departure"

A COMPARISON OF THE Academy's first board in 1805 with the board that commissioned the 1871 building clarifies the changing cultural setting of Philadelphia from the early mercantile republic to the industrial age. The first board was largely drawn from the transactional and negotiation culture of financiers, lawyers, and merchants, the creators of wealth in the age of transatlantic trade, who intended that the new institution would ornament and promote their city. In December 1872, when board member Caleb Cope addressed the dignitaries at the cornerstone-laying ceremony for the present building, he was a representative of the earlier class of board member, having made his fortune as a silk merchant and as the president of the city's largest financial institution, the Philadelphia Savings Fund Society. His remarks contrasted the first trustees with the industrialists who had already funded the building and whose values would shape the design:

> And now we are about to take a "new departure," to use a familiar
> modern phrase, and, instead of looking to our legal brethren
> for material aid in our enlarged scheme for the cultivation and
> advancement of Art, we must depend upon those whose different
> calling in life has led to the accumulation of wealth in their hands.
> Among these the means have been secured to erect upon this
> site the most capacious fire-proof galleries for the reception and
> depository of paintings and sculpture and the instruction in Art
> in our country.
>
> With few exceptions, great fortunes are not made by those
> who practise the law, at least in this city, but they are made by
> those who are called business men, especially by that class who
> are directly or indirectly engaged in the conversion of the raw
> material into useful, and, consequently, merchantable forms.
> It is chiefly the manufacturing interest (more particularly that
> connected with the manipulation of iron which has aggrandized

The mezzanine of the auditorium is carried on a steel beam of bolted
together U-channels, manufactured by the Phoenix Iron Co., supported
by a rolled-steel pipe with a cast-iron capital

A sculpted portrait (fig. 38) in the Academy collection shows him peering out above the folds of a Roman toga, a realistic American face grafted onto forms taken from classical history, rather than the modern portrait of a forward-looking businessman in a suit and cravat, whether on canvas or by photograph. It was a telling image for a board divided between the old and the new.

The discovery in 1864 of a white fungus growing on the Academy's collection when it was stored in the basement during the Annual Exhibitions precipitated the formation of a committee to evaluate the current building, an 1847 classical temple (fig. 39) designed by architect and engineer Richard Gilpin (1812–1887), located on Chestnut Street between Tenth and Eleventh Streets.[14] This had replaced the original premises on the same site, built in 1806 and almost completely destroyed by fire in 1845. Reflecting his dual roles as a member of the board of trustees and a member of the committee of instruction, John Sartain was asked to head the committee.[15] He was joined by fellow board members Claghorn and George Whitney (1820–1885), a manufacturer of locomotive wheels and an art collector.[16] With Sartain's evaluation in hand, the recommendation to the board by the three men was to either enlarge the building or sell its site and erect a new structure that would provide "accommodations exactly adopted to our needs, and also it is hoped, in a style suited to our object and worthy of the city."[17]

The Civil War absorbed both resources and capital for any work on the building, so nothing was done. Three years later, in August 1867, the board returned to the subject, having determined to add a permanent teaching faculty and to become a fully functioning school that would train students in all aspects of the fine arts. At the request of his fellow board members, Sartain laid out requirements that could only be met in a new building at another site:

The space required for the proper accommodation of the Academy is an area of about 100 feet, by 225 feet or its equivalent comprised in other proportions. This, when subdivided into galleries, can be made to yield a wall 2000 feet in length. Nearly 1200 feet of this is wanted for the effective display of the present permanent collection, even without further augmentation, and the remaining 800 feet are calculated for the Annual and other occasional exhibitions. This space is required because these

so large a portion of our industrial people and enabled them to become the patrons of art) upon which we must rely for a liberal support of our Institution in all its requirements. It is quite in harmony with this fact that a gentleman is at the head of the Academy who is an admirable specimen of our successful business men; and who has through his well-attested good character and zealous labor personally influenced the very large subscriptions obtained for the construction of this building.[12]

The new president referred to by Cope was James L. Claghorn, an auction merchant, financier, and art collector who was very much a representative of the old order of mercantile trustees.[13]

FIG. 39 Richard Gilpin, Pennsylvania Academy of the Fine Arts, second building, 1846 (demolished), depicted by John Sartain (1808–1897), engraving and mezzotint on cream wove paper. Although trained as an engineer, Gilpin looked to classical sources rather than the industrial age in his design   FIG. 40 Center Square, Philadelphia, c. 1867. After the demolition of Benjamin Latrobe's waterworks in 1828, William Penn's original central square remained vacant, with railroad tracks crossing through in line with Market Street; only the new Arch Street Methodist Church and Masonic Temple hinted at future urban density

galleries must all receive their light through the roof. The other various wants of the Institution would have to be provided for in a story constructed below the main suite of galleries.[18]

Given Sartain's conclusion that renovations could not meet the expanded goals of the institution, the board directed their search toward a property on Philadelphia's fashionable Broad Street. Their first choice was a free site that would preserve their capital for a new building, preferably on Center Square at the intersection of Broad and Market Streets, the two principal avenues of William Penn's original plan. This site is now buried under the bulk of Philadelphia's City Hall, but in 1867 it was divided by railroad tracks and streets into four landscaped quadrants (fig. 40). The Pennsylvania Railroad's decision to move its freight facilities from the present site of the Wanamaker Building to West Market Street made it possible to imagine new uses for the Square. The Academy proposed as its neighbors the American Philosophical Society, whose collections of books and scientific instruments had outgrown its Independence Square home; the Academy of Natural Sciences, whose recent building on South Broad Street was already inadequate for its growing collections; and the Library Company of Philadelphia, which, although grappling with the explosion of publications in an age of cheap paper and mechanized printing, still held

on to its membership barrier as a means of guarding its social status.[19] While hoping for a site on Center Square, the board hedged their bets by purchasing several properties facing its southwest side. Unfortunately, they were not contiguous. The popular vote to build the new City Hall on Center Square, instead of utilizing the previously selected design that would have surrounded Independence Hall on three sides, ended the dream of free land and raised the price of the holdout properties that the board needed to complete their parcel.

At the center of the battle over the choice of site was mechanical engineer Joseph Harrison Jr., in his dual roles as a member of the boards of the Academy and the newly formed Fairmount Park Commission. With an eye to the proposed Centennial Exhibition that was to be constructed in the west park across the Schuylkill, Harrison suggested that the new Academy building might initially serve as the permanent art building for the Centennial and then be adapted to a school and museum.[20] The distance from the Center City district—where the majority of the teachers, museumgoers, and students lived—to the proposed Centennial grounds proved insurmountable to Harrison's scheme.

＊   ＊   ＊

The connections between the arts and the new engineering culture of Philadelphia took many forms, but were never more directly expressed than in Harrison's poem, "The Iron Worker and King Solomon" (1868), which was privately published by mechanical engineer and Academy board member Joseph Harrison Jr.[21] The booklet's theme was taken from a similarly named painting that Harrison had commissioned in the mid-1860s from Christian Schussele (1824–1879), the Alsatian-born and French-trained artist who had recently taken over the chair of painting at the Academy. The piece was intended to metaphorically represent the connections between engineering and ironwork—Harrison's domains—and the arts, especially architecture. The booklet opens with a photograph of the painting, accompanied by a poem in which Harrison outlined his thesis that the insights of the engineer underlie all architecture:

> Hast thou not asked the Architect,
> Surveyor, Mason, those
> Under whose skillful cunning arts
> This wondrous Temple rose?

FIG. 41 Samuel Sloan, Joseph Harrison Jr.'s mansion, Rittenhouse Square, Philadelphia, c. 1866. Built in 1856 for engineer Harrison, the residence was flanked by office and art gallery wings

The answer to Harrison's rhetorical question was, of course, the mechanic, the prime mover of the engineering culture, who made the instruments for drafting, supervised the design, and crafted the tools for the stone cutting and carving that decorated the structure. In the final stanza, it is the mechanic who sits at the right hand of King Solomon, and who is given credit for the creation of the temple. By the mid-nineteenth century in Philadelphia, mechanics could make that same claim, and many were seated on the boards that directed architectural contracts.

Harrison's commission of the painting paralleled the type of social advancement that residence in the right location offered. Ten years earlier, he had erected a mansion on the east side of Rittenhouse Square (fig. 41), the public park at the heart of Philadelphia's most elite neighborhood. The house was generally Italianate in character, but with massing and detail that Harrison, bolstering his own identity, claimed was based on the architecture of St. Petersburg, where he had made his fortune building locomotives and railroads for the tsar. A notable feature of the house,

and the strongest evidence of Harrison's social aspirations, was the skylighted art gallery that housed his collection in a separate volume adjacent to the main residence. While the house is well known as the work of Samuel Sloan (1815–1844)—also a member of the Franklin Institute—it was particularly remarkable for the integration of iron into its construction. In an aside in his obituary for Harrison that was published in *The Proceedings of the American Philosophical Society*, Coleman Sellers (1827–1927), mechanical engineer and at the time the president of the Franklin Institute, departed from his biographical sketch to comment on Harrison's application of his engineering knowledge to his mansion:

> Of interest it may be to mechanics only, . . . hidden under the plaster of that house are very many ingenious devices to insure stability and to economize space by the use of iron in forms and shapes not commonly known to architects at that time. These were special adaptations suggested by a mind fertile in resources, familiar with the use of iron and possessed of knowledge of how to form it and use it to good advantage.[22]

Christian Schussele (1824–1879), *King Solomon and the Iron Worker* (detail), 1863. Oil on canvas, Pennsylvania Academy of the Fine Arts

* * *

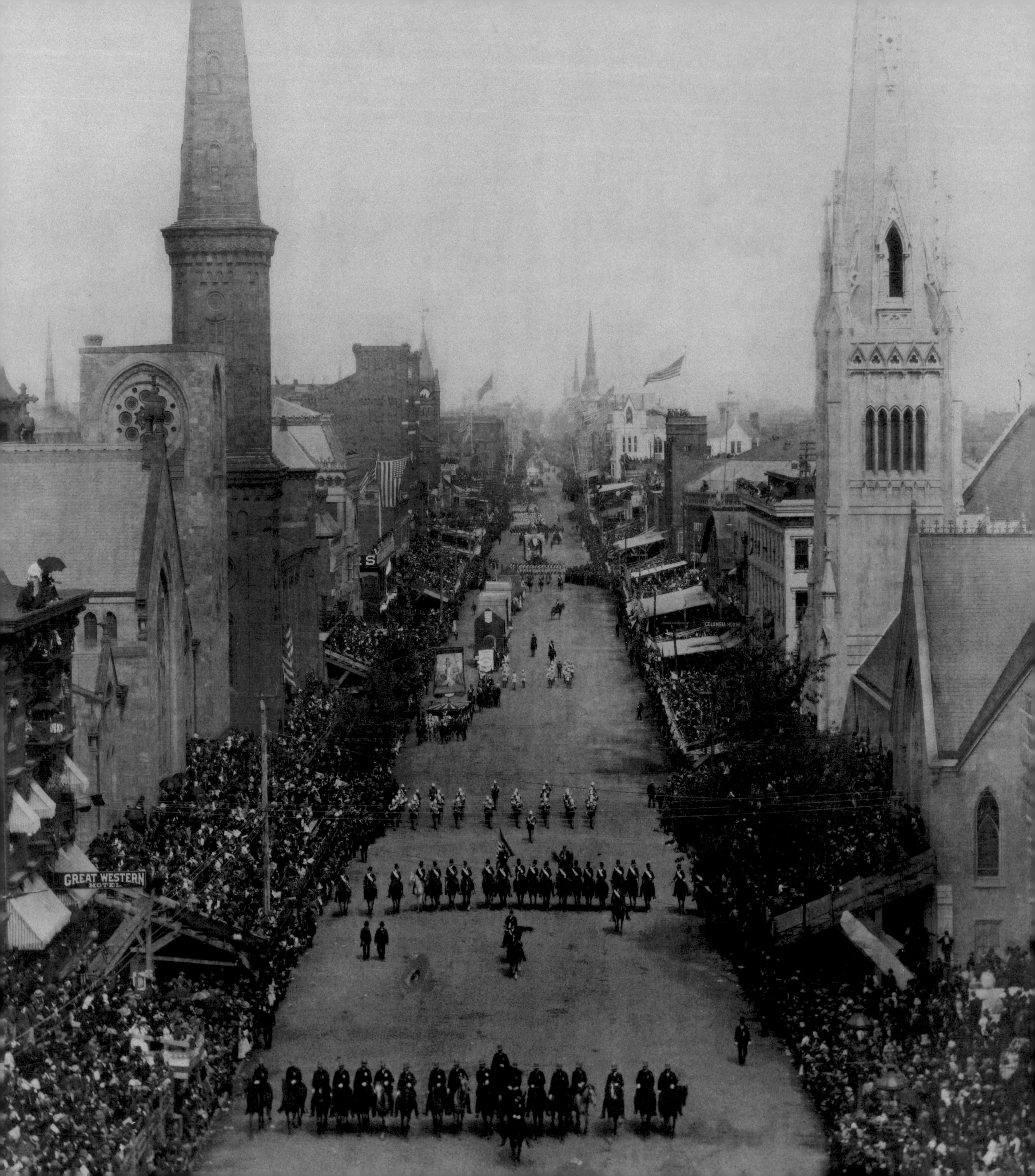
GREAT WESTERN
HOTEL
COLUMBIA HOUSE

The Selected Site

AFTER THE CIVIL WAR, art museums were the question of the moment in leading American cities aiming for metropolitan status. In June 1870, a full year before the beginning of the Academy project, Boston had announced a competition for its recently chartered Museum of Fine Arts. New Yorkers immediately proclaimed a competition for their projected Metropolitan Museum of Art on a site in Central Park. With the coming Centennial celebration offering an opportunity to show off the fruits of their industrial city, the Academy minutes recorded the board's desire to improve Philadelphia's competitive position against its peer cities. Because the Boston and New York projects were already announced, the Academy board determined to proceed immediately with the new building to demonstrate their city's continuing commitment to the arts and to complement the coming Centennial.[23]

By 1871, the board agreed upon a property at Broad and Cherry Streets that provided ease of access and north-facing illumination for the studios. The site almost exactly fit the proportions and size proposed by John Sartain, and its location in close proximity to two important churches, the pre-Civil War brownstone Romanesque revival First Baptist Church and the post-Civil War white marble Puginian Gothic Arch Street Methodist Church, as well as to the nearly completed Norman Romanesque-styled Masonic Temple, offered the likelihood that it would become a part of the city's social fabric. The vision of the Academy leaders was not far-fetched in that the existing churches were, in the spring of 1870, being joined by the brilliantly polychromed, green serpentinite Gothic building for the Lutheran Church of the Holy Communion, designed by the firm then known as Fraser, Furness & Hewitt. Fashionable houses and clubs continued to be built along Broad Street into the early 1880s.

The Broad and Cherry Streets site was purchased over Joseph Harrison Jr.'s strenuous objections, because he feared that the construction of City Hall would produce years of dirt and noise

The civic setting of the Academy, North Broad Street, Philadelphia, with the towers of the Masonic Temple, Broad Street Baptist Church, Arch Street Methodist Church, and Fraser, Furness & Hewitt's Lutheran Church of the Holy Communion (left, unfinished tower), 1887

FIG. 42 Gomery-Schwartz Motor Car Factory, 1916, now the Samuel M.V. Hamilton Building, Pennsylvania Academy of the Fine Arts, North Broad Street, Philadelphia

as well as a change in the tone of the avenue. In the end, Harrison was proven correct; the location was a drag on the institution, first because the construction of City Hall lasted until the end of the century; second, the move of City Hall quickly brought the commercial and financial district to Broad Street, eliminating the mansions, churches, and clubs of the earlier age that had attracted the Academy board. Within a decade of the competition for the Academy, the Pennsylvania Railroad's Broad Street Station was completed on the west side of Center Square, opposite City Hall; by the mid-1880s, office towers and hotels began to encircle City Hall, transforming Broad Street into the new downtown. An unforeseen event was the expansion of the city's metal-crafting industries south from Vine Street, leading, in the early twentieth century, to the construction of an automobile garage with gasoline tanks directly across Cherry Street from the Academy. It was shortly replaced by a multistory automobile facility (now the Samuel M.V. Hamilton Building; fig. 42).[24] Other board members were concerned about the social stigma of locating in the déclassé area north of Market Street.[25] The ensuing battle of words in the minutes and in the boardroom led Harrison, the board's wealthiest member, to resign.[26]

* * *

Fairman Rogers (1833–1900; fig. 43) embodied the energy and potential of the mid-nineteenth-century industrial powerhouse that Philadelphia had become. In an age when people believed in the determinism of ancestry, his biographers pointed out that he was born into a family of mechanics and manufacturers, who shaped his interests and set his course. His father, Evans Rogers (c. 1802–1870), was an iron merchant and manufacturer, board member, and ardent anti-slavery abolitionist; his maternal grandfather and namesake, Gideon Fairman (1774–1827), was the Connecticut-born inventor of an engraving machine used to produce banknotes and fine arts reproductions, who moved his business to Philadelphia and joined the First Unitarian congregation led by the Reverend Dr. William Henry Furness, Frank's father.[27] Fairman's sister, Caroline Augusta, would marry Horace Howard Furness, Frank's older brother.

Fairman Rogers attended the University of Pennsylvania (1853; AM 1856) as it turned from the classical curriculum of literature, philosophy, and history to one focused on the sciences in service to the region's industries. He was the initial graduate of the University's new course of civil engineering, and followed up by taking the school's first advanced degree in the same discipline. After field-work in the United States Coast Survey under Benjamin Franklin's grandson, Alexander Dallas Bache, he returned to a professorship in civil engineering at the University in the Department of Agriculture, Mines, Arts, and Mechanic Arts (essentially the present school of Engineering and Applied Sciences). The department was overseen by trustee William Sellers, the premier machine-tool maker of his time and afterwards head of the University of Pennsylvania's board of trustees.

Like many children of abolitionists, Rogers, despite being married, served in the Civil War. A member of the First Troop, Philadelphia City Cavalry, he was called up for three months of active duty at the beginning of the conflict, but returned to his professorship at the University. During his summer vacations he went back for field service as an engineer, designing temporary bridges in the eastern military theater. Rogers simultaneously managed to give a course of lectures at Harvard, spoke on road and bridge building at the Franklin Institute, and in 1863 was made a founding member of the National Academy of Sciences. There, he served on the committee to solve the problem of compass deviation in the new class of iron warships being built for the United States Navy.[28]

The Franklin Institute reflected his myriad interests in road building and bridge design, magnetism and navigation, photography, glaciers and natural forces, while connecting him to the men most actively involved with the application of the new knowledge of the scientific revolution in Philadelphia. Rogers was a renaissance man for his time, with interests not in old philosophies, but in action, process, and innovation. When he resigned as professor at the University in 1870, after coming into an inheritance on the death of his father, he was sought out by boards such as those of the University and the Pennsylvania Academy of the Fine Arts.

*   *   *

Fairman Rogers's expertise as a civil engineer was likely the impetus for the Howe trusses that carry the roof above the rotunda gallery

FIG. 43 Fairman Rogers in the uniform of the First Troop, from *History of the First Troop, Philadelphia City Cavalry, 1774–1874* (Philadelphia: Hallowell & Co., 1875)

THE BUILDING COMMITTEE

The booklet published for the cornerstone-laying ceremony of 1872 listed the building committee as it existed a year after the original selection.

John Sartain served on the Academy board for twenty-two years, beginning in 1855.[29] An artist and engraver, he made use of the machines invented by Fairman Rogers's grandfather in his reproductions of art. A longtime member of the Franklin Institute, Sartain was particularly interested in modern scientific tools and means of reproduction. In an age of businessmen, he made the art of mass reproduction into a successful business. His connections across the city were apparent in the diverse group of architects whom he would encourage to enter the competition for the Academy's new home.

Matthew Baird (1817–1877) replaced James L. Claghorn on the building committee when Claghorn was elevated to president of the Academy in 1872. A self-taught mechanical engineer who had succeeded to ownership of the city's largest industry, the Baldwin Locomotive Works, on the death of its founder and former Academy board member Matthias Baldwin, Baird was the oldest member of the committee. He had lived a Horatio Alger life, arriving from Ireland as a child, attending Philadelphia's public schools, and attaining advanced training as the assistant to Alexander Dallas Bache, the professor of natural philosophy and chemistry at the University of Pennsylvania.[30] At the locomotive works, Baird foresaw the demand for a new scale of production and in 1867, and again in 1870, brought into the business partners who transformed its production methods. This enabled the company to double and then redouble its production, from 124 locomotives in 1869 to 280 in 1870 and 437 in 1873, the year that Baird retired. His architectural tastes befitted his age. He commissioned his contemporary, Stephen Button (1813–1897), to design his home on North Broad Street, adjacent to his factory. Button, though very much an early Victorian in style, was in demand as an architect for railroad stations and hotels at railroad-developed resorts, and was an early adopter of cast iron as a facade material for buildings, including the Spring Garden Institute a block from Baird's house.

Henry G. Morris, who trained as a civil engineer, was the son of an industrialist and partner in one of the city's great iron works,

Morris, Tasker & Co. He attended Haverford College (class of 1854) at the moment when it was adding engineering and science courses to its former array of classical studies. Metallurgy and the strength of steel became particular interests in his initial work manufacturing steel pipe, and later when he operated the city's largest pump manufactory, the Southwark Foundry. He, too, was a member of the Franklin Institute, an early member of the city's Union League, vice president of the American Society of Mechanical Engineers, and president of the Engineers' Club.[31] By the 1890s, he was co-inventor of an early electric automobile, the "ElectroBat," which won the gold medal for efficiency in the *Times Herald* Motocycle [*sic*] contest in Chicago in November 1895, a seminal event in the development of the automobile. Morris brought knowledge of contemporary metallurgy to his role as board member.

Henry C. Gibson headed a whiskey distillery and attained fame as an art collector.[32] While his collection was typical of the day—encompassing the continental artists but focused on the French school, Thomas Couture (1815–1879), the sentimental realists Jules Breton (1827–1906) and Jean-François Millet (1814–1875), and the ubiquitous Jean-Baptiste-Camille Corot (1796–1875)—his taste in architecture was more adventurous. The year before the Academy competition, he had hired Fraser, Furness & Hewitt as architects for the renovation of his town house at 1612 Walnut Street, which resulted in an interior fantasy inspired by Owen Jones's (1809–1874) Moorish plates. After the split of the firm's principals in 1875, he would continue to hire George Hewitt and his brother William for development projects in West Philadelphia and for his suburban residence, Maybrook. He remained a supporter of the Academy, donating much of his collection to the institution that he had helped transform. Together, the building committee embodied the "new men" referenced by Cope in his introductory talk.

*   *   *

The members of the Building Committee, most of whom came from the industrial and engineering sectors of the economy, would have been comfortable with details drawn from industry to ornament the Academy, such as the drive shafts of the railings of the grand stair

PENNSYLVANIA·ACADEMY·
OF THE
FINE·ARTS·

Furness & Hewitt
Architects

The Competition

THE ARCHITECTURAL SELECTION PROCESS for the new building began with the appointment of the members of the building committee. It would be their professional training, interests, and connections that shaped their choice and in the end would determine the final product.[33] When Joseph Harrison Jr. resigned over the question of the site, Fairman Rogers was offered a seat on the Academy board. In recognition of the applicability of his engineering training to the possibilities of their new building, he assumed the role of chairman of the building committee. As will become clear, without Rogers, the present Academy would not exist.

After the committee was constituted, the minutes reported that each member advocated certain architects. Caleb Cope, still president of the Academy but not on the building committee, suggested his corporate architect and fellow Quaker, Addison Hutton (1834–1916); Henry C. Gibson proposed Henry A. Sims (1832–1875); John Sartain proposed several architects, including his close friend and associate academician Thomas W. Richards (1836–1911), James H. Windrim (1840–1919), John McArthur (1823–1890), and the German-born and trained partners Collins & Autenrieth. Rogers proposed Fraser, Furness & Hewitt. Viewed from the perspective of each architect's capacity to enhance the project, every potential competitor brought particular advantages. If public funds were to be procured, the architect of the new City Hall, McArthur, might have connections to the city and its politicians. Windrim had proven remarkably successful in manipulating the various medievalizing styles of the day, winning in short order the Masonic Temple and the Academy of Natural Sciences competitions in head-to-head battles with many of the Academy competitors; in

addition, he had recently been given the post of architect for the Girard Estates, another potential source of funds for the Academy. Collins & Autenrieth brought European professional training, as well as connections to several wealthy Philadelphians, notably historian and publisher Henry Charles Lea. For various reasons, but most likely because none had strong board connections, each of these architects bowed out of the competition, though Windrim was interested enough to inquire about the specifications and requirements.[34]

Of those who chose to enter the competition, three firms had claims to the allegiance of at least one member of the building committee. While Sims was invited by Gibson, there is no obvious connection between the two men. Gibson's remodeled house on Walnut Street (by Fraser, Furness & Hewitt) was near several projects by Sims, including the Second Presbyterian Church at 21st and Walnut Streets (fig. 44) that was under construction as the Academy competition began. Though Hutton received his invitation from the Academy president, Cope, he also had strong connections to fellow Quaker and committee member Henry G. Morris. In his former partnership with Samuel Sloan, Hutton had designed Morris's South Broad Street residence and provided plans for his summer residence in Newport, Rhode Island.[35] Richards, elected an associate member of the Academy in 1860, was the favorite of Sartain, and had already benefited from his guidance in winning the competition for the University of Pennsylvania. Fraser, Furness & Hewitt had made their mark in downtown banking architecture and in churches and houses across the city. Frank Furness was related by marriage to Rogers and was designing modifications to Rogers's Rittenhouse Square residence. Within a year or two, the architect and his family would move from his father's household to a house at 711 Locust Street owned by the Rogers estate. Such conflicts of interest were normal in the nineteenth century, when

Furness & Hewitt's competition scheme of 1871, reproduced from a photo-zincograph in *Lippincott's Magazine*, shows the massing largely as built, but with additional sculpted panels of Apelles and Phidias and the construction issues of the means of supporting the Cherry Street side unresolved

The Church Building, corner Twenty-first and Walnut streets.

FIG. 44 Henry A. Sims, Second Presbyterian Church, 21st and Walnut Streets, 1869–72. The perspective shows Sims looking to English Gothic sources, with the never-completed spire intended to focus the composition   FIG. 45 Peter B. Wight, National Academy of Design, New York, c. 1861–65 (demolished). Wight's design looked to the North Italian sources advocated by English critic John Ruskin as the best work of the Middle Ages

boards tended to choose from those whom they already knew and trusted. The test for the committee's ability to weather these conflicts would come when they actually had to make the decision on the architect and follow through with the building.

After the selection of the building committee, the next step was the drafting of an architectural program that laid out the sizes and relationships between the various spaces with an eye to the specifics of the new school and the galleries. Again, Sartain was called on to draft the document, with the goal of a "fire-proof" structure—reflecting that fire had destroyed the first building—that would, like the second building, provide top-lighted galleries, as well as a school with studios for traditional drawing from classical casts and smaller studios for life drawing classes. The board meeting of June 19, 1871, ordered letters and copies of the program be sent to the selected architects with a date of November 1 for submission of plans, elevations, and sections, all at a scale of half an inch to a foot, that would result in mammoth drawings roughly 11 feet in length for the 265 feet of the side elevation, the ground and gallery floors, and the longitudinal section. Two additional drawings were

required for the front elevations, one showing a scheme in economical brick and the other in marble, presumably reflecting the desire to compete with New York's National Academy of Design (fig. 45).[36] The relatively long time given for the preparation of the drawings, nearly four and a half months, is especially telling. Similar competitions for churches, such as the almost exactly contemporary project for Boston's Trinity Church, usually provided little more than a month between announcement and submission. Where church designs were relatively formulaic, the committee clearly intended that its competitors would have adequate time to research similar institutions, and, if necessary, to invent a new type of building to serve the hybrid purpose of school and museum.

∗   ∗   ∗

Furness & Hewitt, *Elevation on Broad Street*, c. 1872. The Broad Street facade was largely developed by the time this drawing was made for an exhibit at the Union League of Philadelphia. The tan flap above the doorway provided an alternative for the detail of the main front window

The Choices

WITH THE INVITATION FOR ENTRIES sent to the selected architects, there was no further report on the competition in the board minutes until November 1, when the designs were due. This is not to say that all was quiet during that period. The two younger members of Fraser, Furness & Hewitt had taken the opportunity presented by the competition to sever their relations with the senior member of their firm, John Fraser, who was in Washington, DC, looking for government work. Fraser was nearly a generation older than his partners, a gulf made larger by their relative ages in 1871. Fifteen years earlier, it was Fraser who had, in Frank Furness's unflattering phrase, taught him "the use of the instruments," presumably the craft aspects of basic drafting techniques, but gave him no vision as to the possibilities of the profession. It would have been difficult for the younger architects to assert their own identities, or to express the forces of the new age in which they were living, while under the thumb of the backward-looking Fraser. When he returned to Philadelphia and found himself excluded from the competition, he wrote a letter on the firm's letterhead, but with Furness's and Hewitt's names crossed out, asking that he be permitted to enter a design.[37] Whether because his letter came in October and the board did not feel that he would have time for an adequate response, or because Rogers's real interest was in the younger members of the office, Fraser's request was denied.

The day after the schemes were submitted to the Academy, the internal battle within the committee became evident in a private letter from John Sartain to his favorite, Thomas W. Richards:

> [It] remains to be seen . . . whether you or Furness erect the building. I am bent on having you if I can do it . . . (and conscientiously too). But alas! I give not a cent of money, while Fairman Rogers no doubt gives thousands—more or less, perhaps, according to circumstances.[38]

Although we know but little of two of the submitted projects, Henry A. Sims's plans and elevations survive in the Academy archives in the form of a photographic booklet accompanied by

Henry A. Sims, photograph of original ink and wash competition drawing for Pennsylvania Academy of the Fine Arts, 1871. Broad Street elevation

a text of his analysis for the choices of materials and the plan (p. 62 and fig. 46). His scheme was in the Venetian Gothic style as advanced by British critic John Ruskin (1819–1900), and he may also have been aware of Sturgis & Brigham's recent winning competition design for Boston's Museum of Fine Arts (fig. 47) in a flamboyantly polychromed and decorated Venetian Gothic mode. Sims's front and side elevations were enlivened by sculpted panels along the walls of the gallery level that made evident its purpose as a museum; his design was to be crowned by a gigantic drum and dome above the central gallery crossing—modeled on the Pisa Baptistery of St. John—which was intended to contain a pantheon of great Philadelphians. It would have met the standards of the day as representing a specific historical style and expressing the building's purpose through its sculptural program; however, a closer look revealed that the dome and its necessary masonry core drove the entire plan, distorting the galleries and the teaching spaces.

Nothing of Richards's scheme survives, though it can be assumed that it bore some relation to his design for the new University of Pennsylvania buildings (fig. 48), perhaps a colorful rendition of Academic Gothic with windows sized to the differing purposes of the exterior and certainly adhering exactly to the program for the interior of his patron, Sartain. Of Addison Hutton's scheme, the only evidence is a tiny thumbnail sketch in the architect's daybook for October 5, 1871 (fig. 49), showing the core of the building occupied by a monumental main stair and surrounded by galleries.[39] The masonry cells of the gallery level would have been reflected in similar spaces on the ground floor and carried down to the basement foundations.

There was certainly more than a little horse trading in the two weeks before the final decision and when the vote came, it resulted in the worst of all possible situations, a tie between Sartain's favorite, Richards, and Rogers's favorite, Furness & Hewitt. Rogers reported on the process and its results to the larger board:

> Your committee are [sic] unable to recommend to this Board the adoption of any one of the plans as a model to build from. Of the two that are certainly the best, neither, judged as a whole, interior and exterior combined, should be preferred, because each possesses advantages peculiar to itself, not found in the other. All are

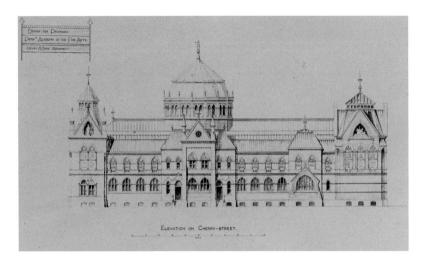 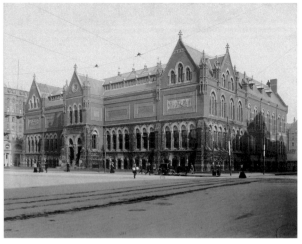

FIG. 46 Henry A. Sims, Pennsylvania Academy of the Fine Arts, 1871, photograph of ink and wash competition drawing. Like the Boston project, Sims looked to northern Italy, with a Pisa Baptistery-style dome atop a vaguely cathedral-like volume in a florid confection of brick and terracotta ornament   FIG. 47   Sturgis & Brigham, Museum of Fine Arts, Boston, MA, 1871–76 (demolished). The Boston architects' richly ornamented scheme displayed the purpose of the building in its Venetian Gothic style and sculpted panels

agreed however that the third best is that of Mr. Sims, and that it is therefore entitled to the premium thereto belonging.

Having now obtained all that can be expected from a competition and with the result stated, we deem the best of further procedure would be to select an architect from among the competitors, and secure his services at such a rate of compensation as the two contracting parties may agree on. No one of the gentlemen has seen the designs of the others during the time they have been in our possession, and they will be returned to their respective authors without an opportunity being afforded.[40]

A bit of deduction suggests how the voting must have played out. Rogers certainly voted for Furness & Hewitt and Sartain obviously voted for Richards. It is likely that Sims held on to the vote of his advocate, Henry C. Gibson, thereby garnering third place. We know from Hutton's day book that, as late as early October, he was still at a rudimentary sketch-plan stage. Sims's competition entry shows the extraordinarily detailed front and side elevations, plans, and sections, and makes it likely that Hutton's preoccupation with other projects meant that his Academy scheme did not match up to those of his fellow competitors. This left James L. Claghorn and Henry G. Morris as the votes that determined the tie. Perhaps Claghorn voted with his school director, leaving Morris to side with his fellow engineer. In any event, after the initial tie, Gibson clearly

shifted to the architects whom he had hired for his house, and Furness & Hewitt won the day by the slimmest of margins.

Rogers's report continued:

Resolved—that the Committee, being unable to agree on either of the plans submitted, return them to their respected authors, and that we award the third premium to that which we consider the third best plan, and the balance of the fund in equal sums between the best two, namely those by Furness and Richards.

Resolved—that Messrs. Furness and Hewitt be appointed architects to the Academy, provided such arrangements as to compensation &c can be agreed on between the academy and the architects named as may be mutually satisfactory.[41]

Thus Furness & Hewitt were awarded the commission, but on the condition that a portion of their prize fee would be shared with Richards. The story picked up again a month later with the board's approval of the decision:

The Committee on Building reported that they had, in conformity with instructions from this Board, entered into an arrangement with Messrs. Furness & Hewitt, to act as architects to the Academy for the sum of $6000 less $400 already paid. For this they engage to prepare plans and drawings for the new Academy of the Fine Arts Building that shall be satisfactory to the Directors,

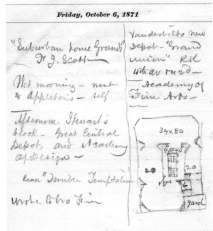

FIG. 48 Thomas W. Richards, University of Pennsylvania Collegiate Building, Philadelphia, 1870–73. Richards used the polychrome Academic Gothic style for many of his projects   FIG. 49 Addison Hutton, daybook page for October 5, 1871, with notes on work in New York and thumbnail-sketch plan for the Academy with a central stair surrounded by the main galleries

will make full and complete working drawings, fully superintend and direct the construction of the building throughout to its final completion.[42]

In early January of 1872, the building committee met again, this time in the newly finished residence of Gibson. The fact that they were meeting in a house designed by Furness & Hewitt was doubtless a positive for the young architects, but the board nonetheless asserted their authorship of the plan and required changes to the Furness & Hewitt scheme:

A Plan of the two ground floors suggestive of an arrangement of rooms and galleries convenient and suited to the requirements of the Academy were [sic] submitted by a member of the committee [Sartain], and after examination and mature consideration, were adopted, and Messrs. Furness & Hewitt the architects who were present, were requested to prepare plans for the Academy building in general accordance therewith [figs. 50A–B], but with the following changes adopted on motion of Mr. Gibson. After arriving at the landing at the head of the first main flight of stairs, a third flight, to be added ascending from it westward into the sculpture gallery, in addition to the two flights already provided ascending to the right and left eastward. Also that the risers of steps should be six inches.

The board's changes were crucial to the success of the project and suggest a knowledgeable client group with sophisticated insights. The opening through the rear wall of the front gallery and grand stair brought the light of the main gallery into the view of those entering the front door, while the reduction of the risers of the steps from seven to six inches caused the need for additional steps that pushed the stair forward toward the lobby (figs. 51–52). In *Complexity and Contradiction in Modern Architecture*, Robert Venturi pointed out the stair's seeming errors against convention —it was too big for its space; it was blocked by a post in the main portal that in turn was narrower than the stair. However, as Venturi observed, it is this quality of bigness that makes the stair both ceremonial and functional while relating it to the outside scale of Broad Street.[43] The stair became, in effect, a giant piston that energizes its hall, while also forming a barrier to force the visitor toward the galleries, thereby screening the private zone of the studios and the school.

∗　　∗　　∗

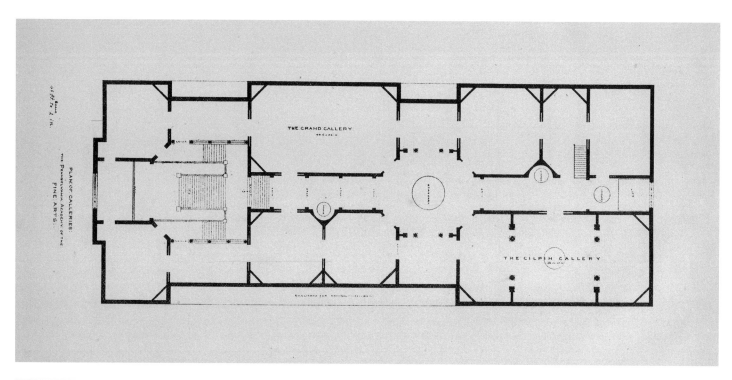

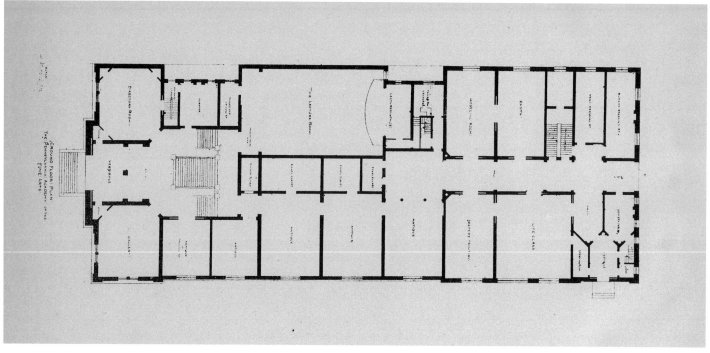

FIG. 50A–B The arrangement of spaces on the studio and gallery floors shown in *Lippincott's Magazine* in 1872 largely persists to the present

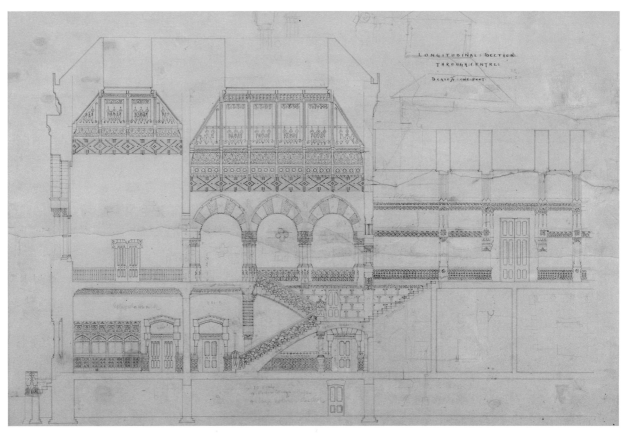

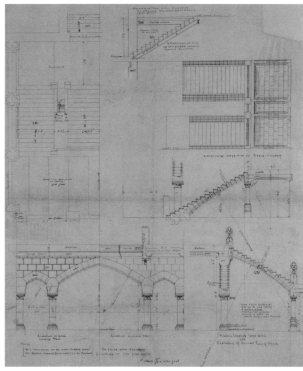

ABOVE   FIG. 51 Furness & Hewitt, *Longitudinal section through centre*, c. 1872.
This slice through the middle of the building shows the sequence from the main
entrance (left) up the great stair to the galleries. The architects intended to
ornament the walls above the Gothic arcade in patterned brickwork and to stencil
the ceilings; in the end, the walls were hung with cast-plaster ornaments and the
ceiling painted a rich blue with gold stars

RIGHT   FIG. 52 Furness & Hewitt, *Details of Main Stairway*, c. 1872. The drawing
reflected the board's request that the main stair continue directly into the long
gallery with the risers reduced from seven to six inches, thus pushing the first run
of the stair toward the entrance

Creative Friction

BEFORE THE QUESTION can be answered as to how the final design was achieved, there is the central question of authorship of the Academy design. The standard answer is either Furness & Hewitt, or Furness alone. It was Frank Furness, after all, who would go on to blaze a trail of individuality for the next generation, and lived on in the memory and the works of his special students, notably Louis Sullivan, then William L. Price, and eventually George Howe (1886–1955). Over time, George Hewitt's designs became more conventional, referencing historical styles for private commissions such as Henry C. Gibson's Scottish castle in the Philadelphia suburbs, Maybrook (1881; fig. 53A); city attractions like the Bourse, near Independence Hall; and, in the early twentieth century, South Broad Street's landmark, the Bellevue Stratford Hotel (fig. 53B).

Sullivan's *Autobiography of an Idea* provides an eyewitness account of the two men as the building construction was underway.[44] In the fall of 1872, Sullivan entered the new architecture program at the Massachusetts Institute of Technology (MIT) that was directed by William Robert Ware, Furness's schoolmate in Richard Morris Hunt's New York atelier in the years immediately before the Civil War. Just as Furness arrived at Hunt's school as a teenager, so too had Sullivan arrived at MIT; but the world of 1872 was already vastly different from the end of the mercantile/fashion age of the 1850s, when Hunt's teaching had been provocative and original. Sullivan hoped to study the new materials, technologies, and possibilities of his moment, but all he got at MIT was warmed-over Beaux-Arts, seen through the lens of an imitator of Hunt. After his first year he abandoned MIT and headed for New York to see if the real Hunt offered more than his student. In New York, Sullivan was shown around by "Stratton" (Sidney, 1845–1925), who sent him on to Philadelphia and Frank Furness's office.

Sullivan followed Stratton's advice, but determined to see Furness's designs for himself before making a decision. After finding examples of the firm's works scattered around Philadelphia, he went directly to their source, climbing the stairs to the office at 3rd and Chestnut Streets. There he found the office principals, whom he captured in a few sharp details. George Hewitt was "a slender,

FIG. 53A G. W. & W. D. Hewitt, Maybrook, home of board member Henry C. Gibson in Lower Merion, PA, 1881. Gibson continued to commission the Hewitt brothers after their split with Furness in 1875   FIG. 53B Bellevue Stratford Hotel, South Broad Street, Philadelphia, 1902–04, 1910–11. Three years before New York's Plaza Hotel opened, hotelier George Boldt, manager of the Waldorf-Astoria, commissioned the Hewitts to design the Bellevue in the modern French manner

moustached person, pale and reserved who seldom relaxed from pose," while Furness was the opposite, "a curious character" who "wore loud plaids, and a scowl and from his face depended fanlike a marvelous red beard, beautiful in tone with each separate hair delicately crinkled from beginning to end." Sullivan's description set up the dichotomy between the two men, with their visually expressed identities paralleled by their opposing approaches to architecture. Hewitt had his nose in books, valuing all things English. It was he who did the "Victorian Gothic in its pantalets, when a church building or something was on the boards." The brash and bold Furness, on the other hand, "made buildings out of his head." That suited Sullivan better. As a corollary to his own original mode of work, which he practiced for nearly half a century, he remembered Furness as a remarkable freehand draftsman who had him "hypnotized, especially when he drew and swore at the same time."[45] When he left the Furness office in the late autumn of 1873, in the depths of the financial crash brought on by the failure of Jay Cooke's railroad speculations, Sullivan had learned a new method of design. In his early work in Chicago, it was Furness whom he would remember and from whom he would borrow, while the inspiration he had received would guide him for the next half century in his ground-breaking Chicago and

mid-American buildings and be revisited at the end of his career in his brilliantly colored jewel-like banks across the Midwest.

Sullivan's account places us in Furness & Hewitt's office at a critical moment after the two young men had separated themselves from lead partner John Fraser and set up their own method of working. The architectural evidence of other buildings undertaken

FIG. 54 Instead of the usual linear sequence of triglyph, metope across a Doric temple, the architects stacked the metopes above the triglyphs and further departed from the classical model with violently colored brickwork

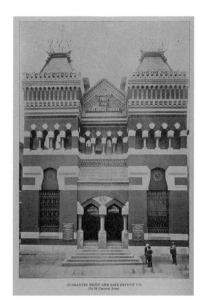
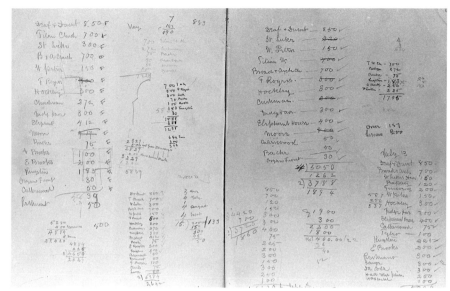

FIG. 55 Furness & Hewitt, Guarantee Trust & Safe Deposit Company, Philadelphia, 1873–75 (demolished). The architectural polychromy and Gothic detail of the Academy design was adapted to this commission on the city's "Bankers Row" FIG. 56 Frank Furness, notebook page, c. 1875, allocating projects by author and fees

by Furness & Hewitt in the first year or two of their partnership suggests, in certain instances, an unusual sharing of design responsibilities, often on the same project. It is as if each overdrew and revised the other's schemes, thus bringing together two minds, one more conventional, one more original, with the resultant complication and interplay of the architectural possibilities of the moment. Yet in other instances, it seems clear that one partner or the other handled the project. Ironically—or perhaps intentionally—Sullivan did not mention the largest and most important commission in the office, the Academy, which was then well out of the ground and rising to the level of the exterior trusses, which would have been installed while he was in the office. Did he ignore this work because it countered his description of architecture as a solo voice, rather than a duet?

The initial schemes for the Academy are evidence of the pair, a duet with bold moves overlaid with delicate conventional detail. On the Broad Street front are the striking hash marks of the Neo-Grec and polychromed brickwork (fig. 54), learned by Furness in Hunt's studio, that vie with Gothic details and traceried windows that certainly came from Hewitt's training in the office of his mentor, John Notman. Shared responsibility is further suggested by the presence of both architects at the initial job meetings, after

which they alternated in the first years of the construction. Similar design characteristics combining radically new ironwork, bold ornamental passages with delicate details from the Gothic Revival, and architectural polychromy appear in commercial projects such as the Guarantee Trust & Safe Deposit Company offices at Third and Chestnut Streets (fig. 55), adjacent to Carpenter's Hall.

The pressure of the economic downturn that forced the office to send Sullivan on his way in the fall of 1873, and differences of professional direction between the two men that are evident after 1875 when the partnership ended, suggest internal conflicts that could not be resolved. Furness's notebooks attest to his growing resentment of Hewitt as he made lists of projects and fees (fig. 56) brought to the business by the partner who initiated each job. Furness, with his extensive network of family and friends, was bringing in a far larger volume of work and most of the fees, while the partners were presumably splitting the profits. By 1875, it was Furness alone at the job meetings and, by year's end, the architects had gone their separate ways. In February 1876, it was Furness who was cited as "architect of the building" in the building committee minutes, and who was charged with getting the sculpted panels made for the front facade; and it was Furness who was generally given credit—or blame—when the building opened.

*　*　*

Band of TILE

Pattern in Black Brick

"Comparatively Unsolved Difficulties"

BEFORE THE CONFLICT between the partners arose, most of the major design decisions had been made and the building began its four-year course toward completion (figs. 58–59). A year after the competition, with the foundations and masonry vault under the first floor completed and the walls rising from the ground, Fairman Rogers summarized the history of the project in a text for the cornerstone ceremony. He concluded with a remarkable statement:

> Partly for commercial reasons, but mainly because it is desirable, in a building the construction of which must occupy a considerable period, to have the longest time for the study of those problems which present themselves, the system of working by separate contracts has been adopted [fig. 60], and we are therefore yet free to decide upon such plans for the roof, the sky lights, and the artificial lighting of the galleries as a careful consideration of these comparatively unsolved difficulties in the construction of art galleries may point out.[46]

There is no other such statement about another principal public building of the period. In Philadelphia, and with the rising tide of innovations in building practices, Rogers proposed to continue to explore new possibilities, even as the construction progressed. The building design process was to be as original as the building. While we have no direct statement about the issues that were under discussion and led Rogers to make his statement, there is good evidence in the sequence of orders for the construction materials of the building. As the cornerstone was being laid, the iron beams that would carry the shallow brick vaults of the second story had just been ordered. Schematic plans for the layout of the iron beams (fig. 57) exist, which in their directness and lack of polish were certainly the work of the iron contractor's engineers and not the architects. Iron was an essential element that would be expressed in the construction of the building, and as we know from the lobby

and other first-floor spaces, it would be visible. The principal problem of the scheme, how the upper wall would be carried above the glass roofs of the studios, had been hidden in shadow in the perspective of early 1872 (fig. 58). It was still unclear in the large one-quarter-inch to the foot scale elevation drawing of the Cherry Street facade that was exhibited at the Union League at the time of the cornerstone laying ceremony in December 1872 (fig. 59). There, the means by which the upper wall would rise above the glass roof of the studio was only suggested by a line of decoration— whether masonry or iron, the structure that would carry the wall had yet to be designed.

In February 1873, a full year after the cornerstone ceremony, the committee, led by Rogers, determined that the pieces of hammered glass for the sloping skylight roof above the studios would be limited to ten feet, a stock size.[47] One month later, in March, another important decision was made—the gallery wall above the studios would be carried on four sets of iron trusses that would be manufactured by the Phoenix Iron Works. An undated ink on linen drawing entitled *Section through the Antique Galleries* (fig. 61) shows the pair of steel trusses supporting the masonry of the upper gallery wall. Presumably, these issues had been under discussion from the moment that Furness & Hewitt received the commission. After all, the set-back wall of the gallery that permitted the continuous skylight above the studios—the engine that drove the entire design—required either a supporting masonry arcade that would block the light to the studios, or a structure of this sort to carry the upper walls.

How did such a device materialize? Given that there is nothing like it in the firm's previous work, the obvious answer lies in a collaboration between the architects and bridge engineer and committee chair Fairman Rogers.[48] Did he push to hire Furness & Hewitt because he thought that the young architects might be most susceptible to the creation of a new type of structure that would best serve the Academy? With Henry G. Morris's knowledge of the metallurgy consistent with the use of iron pipe in a pioneering way as the equivalent of a modern lally column, and with Rogers having made a specialty of bridge design in his teaching and

Furness & Hewitt, *Elevation on Cherry Street* (details; see also p. 74): Top, c. 1871, suggests an initial attempt at rendering the long wall; the second, more finished drawing, 1872, uses a band of ornament to suggest the future line of the still-unresolved structural system along Cherry Street; the modern photograph shows the solution, a steel truss spanning the Cherry Street facade

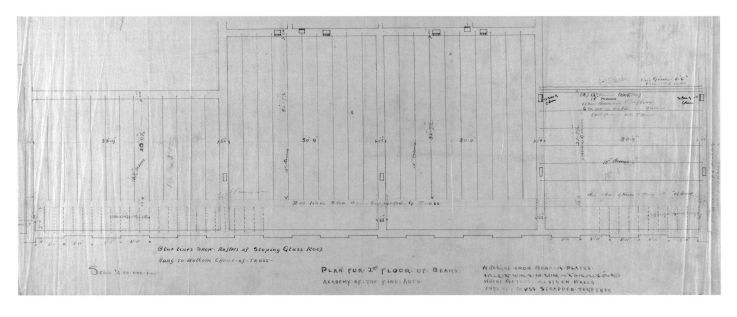

Blue lines show Rafters of Sloping Glass Roof.
Hung to Bottom Chord of Truss.

Scale ¼ to one Foot.

PLAN FOR 2ND FLOOR OF BEAMS
ACADEMY OF THE FINE ARTS.

WROUGHT IRON BEARING PLATES.
WHERE ENDS OF TRUSS REST ON WALLS
ENDS OF TRUSS STRAPPED TOGETHER.

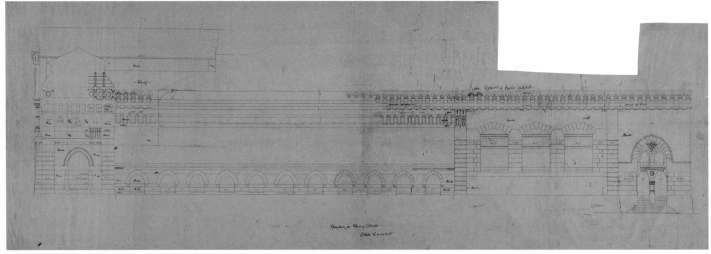

Elevation on Cherry Street

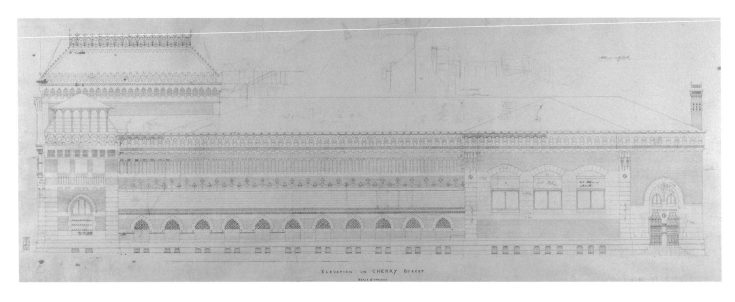

ELEVATION ON CHERRY STREET

FIG. 57 Clarke & Reeves, Phoenix Iron Works (1871–84), *Plan for Second Floor of Beams*, c. 1873. Engineer's drawings were typically far less finished, communicating purpose in a limited vocabulary of lines and washes that here represent the sizes of the steel and the directions of the span; dotted lines show the rafters for the skylight above the studios

FIG. 58 Furness & Hewitt, *Elevation on Cherry Street*, c. 1871, shows the uncertainties of the design, with the central gallery undefined in length and the roof skylights and monitors undrawn

FIG. 59 Furness & Hewitt, *Elevation on Cherry Street*, c. 1872. The exhibited drawing showed the proportions of the front block of the building, the transition to the loft-like volume that housed the galleries above and teaching studios below; pencil notes, added later, show the first elements of the roof-ventilating monitor

FIG. 60 Furness & Hewitt, *Detail Drawing of Stone Work*, c. 1872. The linen drawing of the front stonework was used for blueprints that enabled a stonemason to cut and lay out all but the most complicated of features and told the builder where each piece was to be placed

FIG. 61 Furness & Hewitt, *Section through the Antique Galleries*, c. 1873. In the first three years of construction, the building systems evolved from massive masonry vaults in the basement to minimalist steel and glass, anticipating the modern skyscraper. The paired trusses under the gallery wall on the right mark the moment when the steel truss solved the problem of the gallery above the skylight

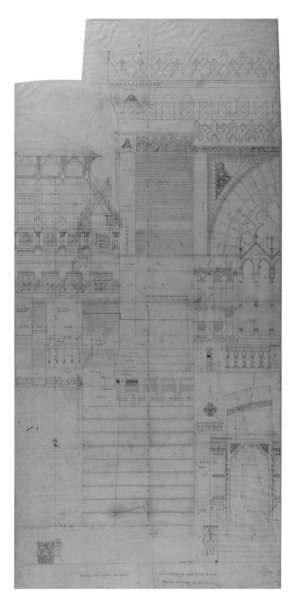

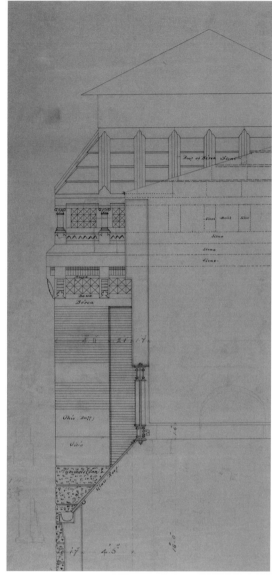

Civil War work—and at least one architect attuned to the idea of an up-to-the-minute architecture for a modern time—the moment was ripe for the application of the possibilities of the industrial age to the special requirements of the Academy. The collaboration between Rogers, Morris, and their architects was possible because it was taking place in Philadelphia, which had become a center of innovative design, first in machines, and, by the 1870s, in architecture.

*   *   *

Antecedents

THAT FRANK FURNESS was primed for such a strategy was apparent the year before the competition when his father, the Reverend Dr. William Henry Furness, gave an address to the American Institute of Architects at their 1870 national convention in Philadelphia. There, he called for an architecture suited to the American democracy and to the latest materials and new possibilities of the age. Dr. Furness's lecture drew on ideas that he had discussed extensively with his childhood friend and lifelong associate, Ralph Waldo Emerson, and which formed much of the American background for what would later be called "organic" design. In lectures reaching back to his own Phi Beta Kappa lecture at Harvard, Emerson held that traditional learning was constrained by precedent:

> The book, the college, the school of art, the institution of any kind, stop with some past utterance of genius. This is good, say they,— let us hold by this. They pin me down. They look backward and not forward. But genius looks forward: the eyes of man are set in his forehead, not in his hindhead: man hopes: genius creates.[49]

Emerson countered the failures of traditional learning with the idea of "self-trust," which he asserted was "the first secret of success."[50] To Emerson and Dr. Furness, the American democracy required its own arts, looking to the wonders of nature as expressed in its mountains, rivers, and seashores, and to modern facts of engineering, instead of European history. Such sources would inevitably lead to "a new order," with the result that American arts would be "organic," like nature, ending the "distinction between the fine and useful arts," because "in nature, all is useful; all is beautiful."[51] Frank's father drew from these constituent ideas of American transcendentalism to argue for the possibility of an architecture suited to the materials of the age, one that drew on the "individual liberty" inherent in the nation not yet a century old. But Dr. Furness recognized the inherent difficulty for architects when they served clients who usually took the safe course of adhering to precedent and judging value by

> [W]hether it was old or new. If we have never seen it before, either in buildings, or in print and photographs, we pronounce it

The architects carefully placed glazed roof panels above the skylighted zones of the galleries while using fireproof slate for the blank zones in between the glazed panels

odd; and when we call a thing odd, we find it difficult to see how it can be called beautiful. With all of our freedom, we do not tolerate oddness. We insist, in this country, upon everything's being cut to one pattern.[52]

He concluded by calling on the profession to devise an architecture that would be suited to the American present, using the emergent materials of the age, such as iron:

Shall [not] this homely, solid substance have rights, and will not Universal Liberty, now no longer a dream but a fact, a component of the heart's blood of forty millions of people, no longer a dead letter, but a spirit, a vital principle—will it not demand—will it not create new orders of Architecture? Answer us, gentlemen, please in your works.[53]

Having discussed similar ideas at the family dining table and heard them in his father's sermons, Frank Furness was armed with the ideas and values that would support a radical transformation of architecture and might produce a "new order" formed in "Universal Liberty" and suited to the materials and purposes of the day. In the course of the design development for the Academy, the young architect would discover that its board would accept a new direction because it paralleled their own work and their core values —and in Fairman Rogers, another of Dr. Furness's congregation who had heard these ideas, he would also find a client. In a city whose leaders were comfortable with engineering and innovation, there was an opportunity to design in a forward-looking manner, to overturn rules handed down from the past, and to begin the course that leads inexorably toward modern architecture. By 1873, with the decision to carry the upper Cherry Street facade on the massive exposed steel truss, and to enlarge the rotunda gallery by carrying the roof above it on steel trusses spanning the masonry piers, the Academy design took off in directions that would shape the Furness practice for the next generation (figs. 62–63). The best of his later buildings were generated not from historical sources, but from the logistical logic of the plan and from the expression of the character and possibilities of steel and iron, the definitive materials of the industrial age. In a commercial era, visual excess in pursuit of identity certainly was no vice. Philadelphia in 1873 was poised between the past and the future. Furness's early masterpiece, the Pennsylvania Academy of the Fine Arts, completed in time for the American Centennial celebration, spread the word of the rising industrial culture just as London's Crystal Palace had done a generation before—but instead of being a temporary exhibition hall that could be dismissed as a giant greenhouse or a bit of engineering, the Academy design marked the transfer of the new ideas to the everyday life of an institution. The future had arrived.

*　　*　　*

TOP　FIG. 62　The Howe trusses that span the rotunda, between the masonry piers, carry steel members from which the rotunda skylight is hung

BOTTOM　FIG. 63　The top-lighted galleries bring natural illumination to the hot tones of the *KAWS@PAFA* installation, 2013–14

The New Client and the New Theory of Design

AT THE MIDPOINT in the years between Thomas Carlyle's "Signs of the Times" essay of 1829 and the 1871 competition to design the Pennsylvania Academy of the Fine Arts, stood the iron skeleton and glass sheathing of London's Crystal Palace, built for The Great Exhibition of 1851. Despite nearly universal praise for its design as an exhibition hall, architectural theory for more conventional buildings remained frozen in the past. Unlike Frank Furness's father, who was freed by the radical fusion of Unitarian and transcendentalist principles to advocate for an architecture of ideas and of its moment, the principal British art critic of the day, John Ruskin, argued that the Crystal Palace notwithstanding, expressions learned from the Bible would remain the basis for future design:

> I cannot now enter into any statement of the possible uses of iron or glass, but I can give you one reason why it is not likely that they will ever become important elements in architectural effect. Assuming then that the Bible is neither superannuated now, nor ever likely to be so . . . it will follow that the illustrations which the Bible employs are likely to be **clear and intelligible illustrations** to the end of time [author's emphasis].[54]

Such backward thinking remained a foundation for the traditional arts, even as similarly dated concepts were being challenged by the research and theories of contemporary scientists and inventors. Innovation in architecture required a cultural context that was free from the control of the past; an alternative design theory independent of historical sources; a clientele who were not afraid to stand out from their peers and who sought to present their own identity; and the wealth to commission significant works of architecture. Philadelphia after the Civil War met all of these conditions. Its industries produced vast wealth. Its industrialists were free of social and cultural constraints to determine their own identity, and most of the city's scientists and engineers were free from the contamination of old-learned cultural forms and had the determination to represent their identity and their industries. Further, Philadelphia's mechanical engineers had developed a new design theory that could lead them in the directions that modern life demanded.

FIG. 64 William Sellers & Co., Philadelphia, "rod-planing machine," c. 1860s. Civil War-era Philadelphia machine designers eliminated classical ornament to conceive a new vocabulary of ergonomic forms that reflected purpose

In the decade before the Academy design competition, Philadelphia had become the epicenter of a culture of innovation in the less-studied but foundational field of industrial design. By the 1850s, Philadelphia-made machines (fig. 64) were instantly identifiable by specific design characteristics.[55] Instead of cluttering their machines with classical columns and Gothic panels or highlighting them with gold accents, Philadelphians shaped a design method of continuous refinement toward greater stability and utility. By the 1860s, these ideas had coalesced into a theory and a process that was analogous to Ralph Waldo Emerson's thoughts on fitness and Charles Darwin's theory of natural selection and could be adapted to other fields—particularly architecture. In 1874, the Franklin Institute organized an exhibition of Philadelphia machinery in anticipation of the coming Centennial Exhibition, at which they intended to introduce the city's industrial products to the nation and the world. The exhibition ended with a lecture by Coleman Sellers, the chief machine designer for the machine-tool maker William Sellers & Co., which laid out his company's design strategy:

> I would gladly trace the progress in the arts during the past fifty years, could it be done in the limited time I dare address you, but I would be derelict in my duty were I to fail to do so in one particular instance, because it seems to me great principles are

A rare construction photograph, c. 1874, shows the iron framing of the front mansards in place, contrasting with the traditional masonry spires of the Masonic Temple (right) and the Broad Street Baptist Church (left)

*involved. The machine display in this room is unquestionably very fine, and when one glances over that broad expanse of iron servants of man's will, and peers through the forest of belts that give motion to these machines, **one cannot but be struck by the remarkable uniformity in color there shown, and doubtless may think the dark gray tint, the absence of all gay colors indicative of our Quaker tastes and habits** [Sellers's emphasis]. Ladies and gentlemen, there is to the student of a nation's art progress, more in that quiet color than can be traced to any such reason. The lesson it teaches is worth learning.*

*   *   *

*When machine making became a trade, man still seeking to satisfy his innate longing for the beautiful, borrowed from other arts, regardless of fitness, forms and colors of acknowledged beauty. He called to his aid every type of architecture and decked his Gothic or Corinthian steam engine with all the gorgeous hues a painter's palette could offer him. As man's taste develops by culture he learns that **beauty cannot be separated from fitness** [author's emphasis], that the most graceful forms, the most lovely colors fail to satisfy the eye when transported from their proper sphere or inharmoniously blended. It is an uneducated taste that finds satisfaction in brilliant colors only or seeks to beautify uncouth forms by gorgeous paints, while a **higher culture fashions forms to suit the purpose for which they are designed** [author's emphasis], and colors them in subordination to their uses and surroundings. The grotesque architectural machinery of not many years ago is now seldom seen; conventional forms beautiful enough for some purposes when wrought in wood or stone have been abandoned, so that now, looking over this typical collection of machines for so many varied uses, we find that a **new order of shapes, founded on the uses to which they are to be applied and the nature of the material of which they are made** [author's emphasis], have been adopted and the flaunting colors the gaudy stripes and glittering gilding has been replaced by this one tint, the color of the iron upon which it is painted.*[56]

Three pivotal ideas stand out from Sellers's lecture. First, "*beauty cannot be separated from fitness.*" This was an idea that almost exactly paralleled Emerson's ideas on organic design, as well as Darwin's conclusion that nature's forms, colors, and patterns

were responses to environment and activity. From the first idea follows the second, that "*higher culture fashions forms to suit the purpose for which they are designed.*" A generation later, Louis Sullivan, in his text "The Tall Office Building Artistically Considered," and doubtless recalling his experience in the Furness office, gave a pithier version in his oft-quoted "Form ever follows function."[57] The third idea, "*a new order of shapes, founded on the uses to which they are to be applied and the nature of the material of which they are made,*" adds the criterion of understanding and the expression of material and purpose that should, indeed must, be represented in modern design.

Sellers's theory could be applied to any design field from machinery to architecture, and it provides an explanation for the revolutionary direction taken by the building committee of Philadelphia's Pennsylvania Academy of the Fine Arts, as well as by Furness's later career. Shorn of a dependence on history, and shaped to an evolving understanding of purpose, each machine to be introduced was a critique on the last. In a similar vein, architects could build using and expressing new materials to devise inventive shapes suited to the specific purposes for which they were designed. Furness, freed by his family's belief in self-expression and self-trust, and carrying in his core the Emersonian belief that function and design are expressively related, nonetheless required a clientele who were comfortable with articulating their world. Over the next three decades, Furness would design most of his seven-hundred-plus commissions for engineering-centered businesses: the Philadelphia & Reading Railroad, the Baltimore & Ohio Railroad, and the Pennsylvania Railroad; factories; hospitals that increasingly reflected the impact of germ theory; and private commissions for the industrialists' homes, institutions, clubs, and vacation houses as far north as Maine and south as Georgia.

The Pennsylvania Academy of the Fine Arts was the first of the Furness commissions that rethought a building in its entirety to arrive at a model. Nearly a century and a half later, it still serves its task with distinction. The success of the building was a result of the collaboration between the architects and the board, particularly the three members who brought special knowledge to their project: the school director John Sartain, the bridge engineer Fairman Rogers, and the materials specialist Henry G. Morris. Author Michael J. Lewis suggests that Thomas Eakins also may

have been involved in the design of the skylight system. As an Academy student in the former building who had recently returned from study at the Gérôme studio in Paris, Eakins would have been aware of up-to-date art studios in France, while Rogers's interest in photography could have also played a role in the Academy design, as skylighted studios were a particular interest of photographers of the period, again suggesting a connection between the sciences and the arts.[58] The coming Centennial and the desire to express the rising industrial culture must have also been a trigger in pushing Philadelphians toward a new design strategy, one that was as adventurous as the American Revolution.

In any event, the Academy building would become a testing ground for the use of the materials of the industrial age in a civic structure. Furness's task was to give aesthetic expression to these heretofore industrial components. As these materials were incorporated into the Academy, they appeared in similar conditions and uses in other projects by the firm, most of which can be specifically attributed to Furness rather than Hewitt. Furness first gave expressive character to metal construction in its various states—cast, wrought, and rolled—in the stairs of the Northern Savings Fund and Safe Deposit Company (fig. 65). The bank's stair is similar

FIG. 65 Furness & Hewitt, Northern Savings Fund and Safe Deposit Company, Philadelphia, 1871–72. Details of the bank, designed as the Academy was underway, parallel that project

FIG. 66 Furness & Hewitt, rear stair to mezzanine (replaced with fire stair in 1973–76 restoration). Furness's evocative use of wrought iron for railings suggests the pawls that prevented giant gears from reversing direction

in design and detail to the contemporary iron stair at the rear of the Academy that was ordered in 1872 (fig. 66). By the summer of 1873, when Sullivan was working in the office, the ground floor of the Academy was well underway and the exposed iron columns that would carry the wrought-iron beams to support the east wall of the auditorium had been ordered and presumably installed. The massive steel girders, with rivets bulging across their surfaces, which spanned the auditorium and carried the beams of the fireproof ceiling and gallery floor above, would have been installed at the same time, and must have shocked those accustomed to wood beams and trusses and molded plaster coverings.

In the same months that Sullivan was with the firm, the final details were drawn for the monumental masonry stair leading to the galleries (fig. 67). Both Furness and Hewitt had been trained in the use of masonry as the hallmark of traditional architectural

FIG. 67 For a Beaux-Arts-trained architect, the monumental stone stair was a standard high point of a design

FIG. 68 Furness, Evans & Co., Baltimore & Ohio Terminal, Philadelphia, 1886 (demolished). A decade after the Academy project was complete, Furness designed the concourse of the B&O terminal as a room entirely of steel, glass, and concrete, celebrating the materials of the industrial city

grandeur, so it would not have occurred to them to substitute the lightness and impermanence of steel for the mass and solidity of stone for the steps and the landings. Bids were sought in the summer and the contract was awarded to William Struthers, a former board member and operator of the city's largest stone yard, who began supplying the cut and shaped stones by the beginning of September. In Furness's later projects, iron would replace stone, symbolizing his acceptance of the new age. This change was evident in the concourse of the Baltimore & Ohio Terminal (1886; fig. 68) at 24th and Chestnut Streets; in the entrance tower stair of the University of Pennsylvania Library (1888; fig. 69); the grand stair in the lobby of the Pennsylvania Railroad's Bryn Mawr Hotel (1889, now the Baldwin School); the main stairs of the railroad's Broad Street Station (1892); and on to twentieth-century buildings, including the railroad's Arcade Building (1901) and the passenger station in Wilmington, Delaware (1905; fig. 70). In each of these new buildings, he would turn the stairs into demonstration pieces for the iron age, using steel stringers and treads, wrought-iron railings, and cast-iron newels. Never again would traditional masonry have pride of place.

Yet even stone could be transformed in a modern manner. Toward the end of construction, the Academy commissioned the decorative stone work cladding the walls of the main hallway. Instead of craftsmen carving with chisel and hammer, the marble

slabs of the walls are incised with crisply cut floral and linear ornament that was created by a new sand-blasting technique (fig. 67; see also pp. 45 and 56), invented in Philadelphia by Benjamin Tilghman and licensed to the Struthers Marble Works. It was described in *Johnson's New Universal Cyclopaedia*:

> *Elaborate ornamentation of stone can be secured at a cost which is comparatively insignificant, since the complication of the pattern is entirely without influence. The stonework of the new Academy of the Fine Arts in Philadelphia was all ornamented by the sand blast. Exquisite tracery work has been cut by it out of thin white marble by cutting the pattern half through the slab then reversing and cutting from the other side completely through. The beveled edges of the design meet in the centre of slab and the open tracery thus made when placed before a background of colored marble produces a most excellent effect.*[59]

Rogers had been right in delaying finalization of all the systems. By the end of construction, iron trusses spanned spaces, and machines, rather than the craftsman, had become active makers of the building.

*   *   *

FIG. 69 Furness, Evans & Co., University of Pennsylvania Library, Philadelphia, 1888–90. The stair of the new university library provided a lesson in the various states of iron with cast-iron newels, wrought-iron railings, and rolled-steel girders

FIG. 70 Furness, Evans & Co., Pennsylvania Railroad Station, Wilmington, DE, 1906–08. Into the twentieth century, Furness rejected Beaux-Arts classism to celebrate the materials of the industrial age

Building the Academy: The Panic of 1873

TWO WEEKS AFTER the contract had been signed with William Struthers for the Academy stair, on Thursday, September 18, the nation was hit by the financial panic of 1873, precipitated when Jay Cooke's banking house at 114 S. Third Street, in the heart of the city's banking district, could not meet its debts. Louis Sullivan was in the Furness office, also on Third Street, and heard the buzz from the street that quickly became a torrent of sound:

> One day in September, it was very warm, all windows were open for air, the force was wearily at work. As they worked, there came through the open windows a murmur, barely noticed at first; then this murmur became a roar with wild shouting. Then, all to the windows. Louis saw, far below, not pavement and sidewalks, but a solid black mass of frantic men, crowded, jammed from wall to wall. The offices of Jay Cooke & Co. were but a short distance south on Third street. Word came up that Jay Cooke & Co. had just closed its doors. Louis saw it all, as he could see down both Chestnut street and Third. Chestnut westward from Third also was a solid mass. The run on the banks had begun. The devastating panic of 1873 was on, in its mad career. Louis was shocked, appalled at the sight. He was too young, too inexperienced, to understand what it really meant, even when told it was a panic in finance, that credit had crumbled to dust, that men were ruined, and insane with despair; that this panic would spread like wild-fire over the land leaving ruin in its wake everywhere.[60]

The panic slowed the pace of work for the Furness & Hewitt office and by November required Frank Furness to lay off Sullivan. It also shaped the next phase of the Academy project. By early December 1873, it was reported that the walls were nearly finished and had been covered to protect them during the winter.[61] In January 1874, with costs already exceeding the original budget, the board asked for and received a detailed projection of the amount of work needed to finish the building, as well as of contracts already existing that had been undertaken. The crash had slowed donors' payments to the project, and the trustees were rethinking every aspect of the design to save money. To raise funds, the board offered their contractors the rents from their South Penn Square

The lower stair gallery utilized a rich palette of machine-made Minton tiles for the floor and tile wainscoting for the walls, capped by a band of sand-blasted ornament in-filled with blue mortar

FIG. 71 Steel columns of the second story

properties in lieu of cash payments. The stonemasons, Atkinson & Myhlertz, wrote a terse note to John Sartain:

> *Dear Sir!*
>
> *Yours of yesterday just received. We are very sorry we can not oblige you, but what we want is Cash. Stone is cash, Wages is cash. We could do nothing with Ground rents at present. We hope Mr. Claghorn will oblige us, if he can spare us $1500 more and $1500 in 2 or 3 weeks we will be satisfied. We took the Contract low, our margin is very small, but we looked upon it as a Cash job.*[62]

Because Struthers had a massive income flow as chief stone provider for Philadelphia's City Hall, he was able to take one of the Academy's properties in lieu of payment for his stone work, but progress slowed.

The roof structure was discussed in March 1874, but contracts for the steel and wrought-iron trusses that were to be fabricated by the Phoenix Iron Works had yet to be signed by the following June.

The previous December, the architects had written to Fairman Rogers asking to renegotiate their contracts because, while they saved significant amounts by negotiating with the individual contractors and material suppliers, the additional time entailed by the work had not been assumed in the original contract and the peculiarities of their design required significantly more drawings to communicate the unusual materials and the novel construction strategies.[63] In the context of the fundraising problems, Rogers did not immediately present the request to the board, delaying until June when it was agreed that an additional $1,500, a quarter of their original fee, would be paid the architects to complete the project.

In the spring of 1874, the building committee was investigating the means to construct the curved plaster surfaces of the coved ceilings that would form the transition from the walls to the skylights.[64] The usual method, utilized by John Soane half a century before for the Dulwich Picture Gallery, south of London, was to shape curved wood pieces to which wood lath would be nailed to support the plaster. Having lost its first building to fire, one of the core principles of the Academy design was to be as nearly fireproof as possible, hence the industrial pipe columns and steel girders spanning the rotunda of the second story (fig. 71). The architects also designed an iron bracket (fig. 73) capable of receiving lath made either of wire or wood to carry the plaster of the coved ceilings. The board decided on the iron brackets, but was then faced with the problem of having them fabricated, as it was not a standard product. Three firms were approached: Phoenix Iron, which provided most of the steel beams, wall and roof trusses; "Bement" (William B. Bement & Sons, machine tool makers whose principal was in 1875 a new board member); and "Morris" (trustee Henry G. Morris's plant, presumably the Morris, Tasker & Co. iron works), which produced a broad array of iron fittings to hold piping.[65] Morris's bid was the lowest and therefore accepted.

Finances continued to dog the project. In February 1875, the situation was again dire and it was even questioned whether the building would be finished in time for the May 10, 1876, opening of the Centennial Exhibition. The board again reviewed all contracts and the work that remained to be done. The Philadelphia Savings Fund Society agreed to make a loan against the income that the Academy would receive when it sold its original building

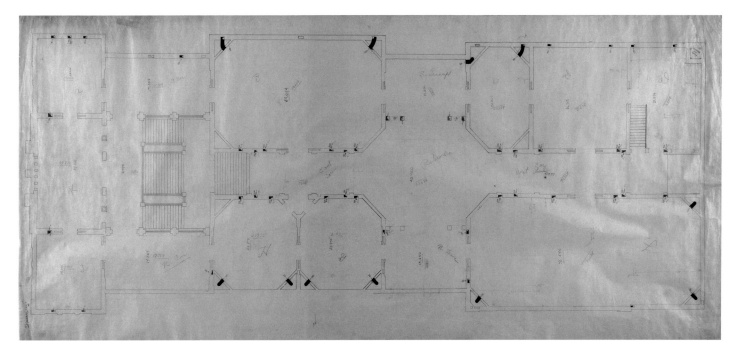

on Chestnut Street. After additional discussion, it was thought better to simply sell the mortgage to the bank, providing $50,000 toward the project.[66]

The impact of the crash on the design can be found in the varied states of the section drawings. The surfaces of the original paper drawings were scraped to remove the ink lines of the first scheme and revised on the tell-tale roughened paper, while linen tracings show ever-increasing simplifications. In the late-1872 drawings for the crossing of the long sculpture gallery, stone walls of carefully cut blocks of stone were to carry mighty arches (fig. 74A). These were redrawn showing pipe columns carrying iron beams (fig. 74B) that supported plaster walls to the skylights. The structural revolution is particularly evident in the details of the rising masonry walls, beginning with the brick foundations of the basement that carried the lower corridor walls and continued as the second story walls that framed the long gallery. Their relatively narrow spacing constrained the desired larger space at the intersection

FIG. 72 Furness & Hewitt, *Second Floor Heating Plan*, c. 1874. The main gallery-level plan was used to direct the heating engineers; red openings indicate heat flow into the space and dark openings mark the return air flow to the basement. In the rotunda, heat was released through the pierced cast-iron column bases (see p. 99)

FIG. 73 Furness & Hewitt, *Metal bracket supporting cove plaster ceiling in gallery and supports for front gallery framing* (detail), c. 1874. In an effort to make the building as fireproof as possible, custom metal brackets were designed and manufactured by Academy trustee Henry G. Morris's firm, Morris, Tasker & Co.

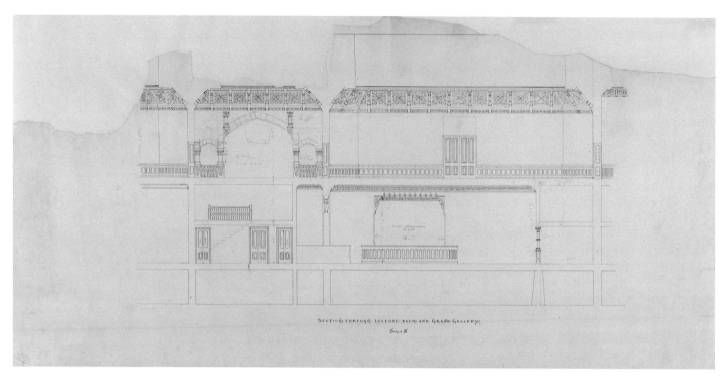

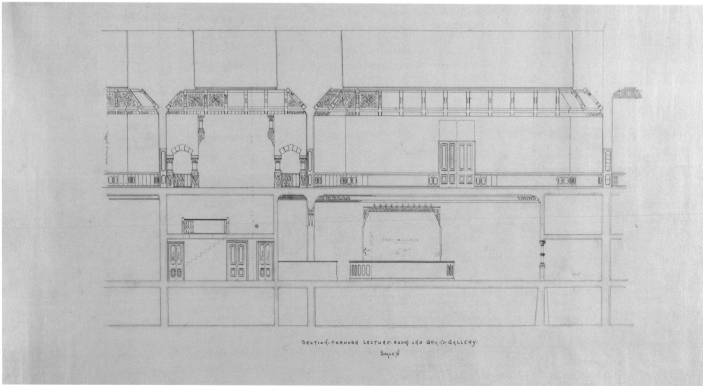

FIG. 74A–B Furness & Hewitt, *Section through Lecture Room and Grand Gallery*, c. 1872. This early section shows masses of ornament in the upper zones of the galleries and a complicated series of stone arches carried on stumpy stone columns to span the cross gallery. The stone structures were eliminated in favor of the more economical and industrial pipe columns and steel girders. In the later drawing, the large spans are replaced by steel but the smaller columns and arches remain. These were entirely eliminated in construction

FIG. 75 When costs became an issue in the economic downturn of 1873, the shift to concrete flooring for the galleries proved a less distracting material than the Minton tile of the first floor

of the east-west and north-south axes of the long sculpture gallery and the crossing galleries. The architects, certainly with the encouragement of Rogers, returned to the device of the Cherry Street facade, employing four pairs of iron trusses to carry the roof trusses above the break in the masonry that framed the corridor. In the main stair hall, economical, mass-produced, cast-plaster tiles were hung over the rough construction-grade brickwork, instead of constructing the entire wall in more expensive face brick laid in a complex pattern in the conventional style for monumental spaces of civic architecture that Furness had learned from Hunt. By the

summer of 1875, it was decided that plain concrete (fig. 75) would be used for the flooring for all spaces but the main stair hall, which would be laid with decorative encaustic tile imported from Great Britain (p. 86). Each of these decisions had the happy advantage of reiterating the industrial character of the building's fresh design, making it such an appropriate part of the Centennial Exhibition's focus on the new forms and materials of the industrial city. By the following winter, final details were being attended to and the building opened on schedule in April 1876, in concert with the opening of the Centennial Exhibition on May 10.

* * *

Learning From the Academy

THE LESSONS TAKEN from the Academy quickly appeared in other buildings across the city designed by Frank Furness's competitors. They, too, were affected by the economic downturn, and doubtless looked for means to achieve thrift in their projects. Nonetheless, the 1873 decision of Furness's erstwhile competitor, Henry A. Sims, to use wrought iron to construct the flying buttresses of the brownstone chapel of ease (fig. 76) for Holy Trinity church was a signal event. Iron had even captured ecclesiastical architecture, the stronghold of traditional design. In coming years, when the heads of Philadelphia's iron and steel businesses were asked for funds to

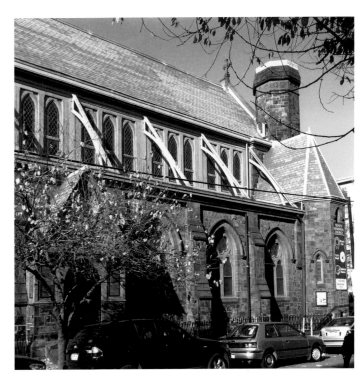

FIG. 76 Henry A. Sims and James P. Sims, Holy Trinity chapel of ease, Philadelphia, 1874. Where Sims had relied on conventional masonry for the Academy competition, by 1874 he had adopted the materials of the industrial age, using exposed steel for the flying buttresses of his Gothic chapel

The delicate trusses of the attic reappeared in Centennial Philadelphia in the light trusses of the Centennial Machinery Hall by Joseph M. Wilson (see p. 18)

FIG. 77 James H. Windrim, Academy of Natural Sciences, Philadelphia, 1868, 1873–76 (reconstructed). Windrim clad the exterior of the new Natural Sciences building in Academic Gothic, looking to Thomas Richards's work at the University of Pennsylvania

FIG. 78 James H. Windrim, Academy of Natural Sciences, Philadelphia, 1868, 1873–76 (altered beyond recognition). The skylighted inner great hall, constructed entirely of exposed iron columns and lintels, was an apt parallel to the skeletons of dinosaurs and other prehistoric creatures

build churches, they would feel free to request that "iron be used and treated as such."[67] Iron was put to an even more remarkable use in James H. Windrim's contemporary scheme for the Academy of Natural Sciences. There, the exterior was of the green serpentinite stone, with sandstone and brownstone trim, and Gothic detail (fig. 77) very much in the manner of Thomas Richards's buildings for the University of Pennsylvania. Instead of distorting iron to the Gothic columns and arches of Deane and Woodward's Oxford Natural History museum of 1859, Windrim framed the new building on Logan Circle entirely with a grid of steel columns (fig. 78), riveted together at their flanges, carrying rolled iron girders with smaller iron beams spanning the bays that in turn carried brick arches and concrete floors.[68] In the principal public space on axis with the main entrance and oriel window, this new structure was the dominant feature. The interior of the Academy of Natural Sciences could have been a factory—except that no factory had yet made the leap to an all-metal armature. By the time that the Centennial celebration began, iron was commonplace across the city, appearing as lintels spanning openings to carriage houses, store fronts, and other structures, as well as forming the columns and framing of the main exhibition and machinery halls of the fair.

While the Academy was being designed and constructed, the same financial events that were playing havoc with its funding transformed the designs for the Centennial fair buildings. After the crash, the vast baroque schemes advanced in the boom of the early 1870s were impossible. By 1874, a new team of designers, led by Pennsylvania Railroad staff engineers Joseph M. Wilson (1838–1902) and Henry Pettit (1842–1921), were assigned to design the main exhibition hall and machinery building (see p. 18). Applying their specialized knowledge, they selected standardized construction systems used in regional mill buildings to construct vast halls that were factory-like in their directness, and in the end were the logical complement to the great machines and industrial products of the fair.

∗   ∗   ∗

FIG. 79 Furness & Hewitt, built-up girder spanning the auditorium. Before rolled steel I-beams were a standard building material, large spans were constructed of flat plates of rolled steel, joined with rivets that gave a muscular character

FIG. 80 Furness & Hewitt, cast-iron capital, wrought-iron shaft, and rolled-steel U-channels bolted together to carry the mezzanine at the rear of the auditorium. Iron could be cast in decorative shapes, like the capital, but Furness used the latest materials of the industrial age with a directness that heralded twentieth-century modernism

Reception

CRITICS ADMIRED the fair buildings and accepted their industrial character as being in the tradition of the Crystal Palace and other transitory structures, but in an era that still looked to history and precedent for permanent civic buildings, they were bewildered by the Academy design.[69] A writer assigned to cover the Centennial Exhibition for the Philadelphia-based *Potter's American Monthly* got around to commenting on the new building six months after its opening, just as the Centennial celebrations were ending. The harshness of his assessment reflected his confusion at its distance from the standard precedents, and set the tone for later discussions of the building:

> *The style of architecture appears to baffle critics; one calls it ornamented Gothic; another modified Gothic; another nearly touches correctly in calling it Byzantine or Venetian, perhaps we may come still nearer the truth in designating it as a combination or patchwork style; we doubt if any known epithet can convey to one who has not seen it a conception of the marvelous incongruities that go to make up the showy exterior of the Academy of Fine Arts—the architect has shown himself a universal genius in architectural art and appears to have been so lost in his admiration of the many approved styles that he did not choose any one; though he affords a suspicion that he prefers the Venetian, he no sooner starts on that style than he appears to repent his choice and modifies until the style loses its right to that class designation.*[70]

The magazine's critic was not alone in his view of the building; even so august a historian and champion of Victorian architecture as Sir Nikolaus Pevsner, who visited the Academy after its restoration for the Bicentennial of 1976, could only describe it as "vintage Furness of the grossest caliber."[71] While the Academy is usually categorized

Frederick Gutekunst, Pennsylvania Academy of the Fine Arts, May 1876.
The first photograph of the completed building shows the Broad Street
front before the name had been carved above the main entrance

97

FIG. 81 Students modeling a musk ox in top-lighted sculpture studio, c. 1904

FIG. 82 Charles Truscott, top-lighted north-facing cast studio, housing casts of the Parthenon sculptures and other statuary, 1890s

as "eclectic," the larger ideas that make it important went unaddressed, presumably because its deviation from the norms of the day was repugnant to the critics, who expected buildings to follow precedent, and none could see beyond the flamboyance to the essence of the design. The critic's response reflected contemporary architectural scholarship/theory that defined, and in the process limited, the concept of historic styles to fixed formulas of elements, proportions, and materials. This left him to muse as Mark Twain might have, with tongue in cheek, piling on absurdities to make his point. Tellingly, the *Potter's* writer completely ignored the new materials and their application to a civic building. He was not alone. At the beginning of the Centennial celebration, the critic for the New York–based *Art Journal* remarked that the "long Cherry Street flank is so monotonous as to cause the leisurely observer a feeling of vague dissatisfaction," but he somehow overlooked the immense, exposed, riveted steel truss running most of the length of the facade that was its principal feature. In addition, he did not comment on the discontinuities of the design, as the lines of the front block were entirely distinct from the lines of the gallery and studio zone, and those of the rear block. Nor did any critic mention, or even appear to notice, the giant roof-top ventilators above the side wings flanking the central mansarded block of the Broad Street front, and the raised monitor that ran the length of the gallery roof.[72] The cultural blinders of the day meant that Frank Furness's obvious references to the machine culture were

overlooked as well. Every critic missed the logistically based planning methods of the modern factory that separated the three main groups of people and materials by their access points: the public entering through the main doors on Broad Street; the art students removed as far as possible from the paying public to their own entrance on Cherry Street; and the giant paintings and sculptures so dear to Victorian taste, together with the horses and cows that would be used as models in the studios (fig. 81), carried by a factory-scaled freight elevator that opened on the rear alley and provided access from grade to first floor and up to the gallery level.

And yet when the *Potter's* critic discussed the interior, he recognized that the Academy was a triumph that brilliantly solved the dual roles of school and museum, providing the best spaces yet devised for creating art in the studios below, and for viewing art in the galleries above:

> But when we have passed the impending triple arch and gotten within the building we forget and forgive the absurdities of the exterior in admiration of the perfect and exact fitness of every part of the interior for its specific purpose; indeed the interior leaves nothing to be desired in the way of modification or change. The first story, devoted chiefly to educational purpose, includes a lecture room forty by sixty feet, a life-classroom forty feet square, with studio for drapery and still life, a modelling-room, a library and print room twenty-four by fifty-four feet; the director's room

and five galleries of casts from the antique averaging more than thirty feet in width each. The exhibition galleries occupy the upper floors and are admirably planned, finished and decorated, while the light is ample and its supply well managed according to the special requirements of the works exhibited.[73]

The writer was apparently oblivious to the new systems of the industrial age that the architects had mastered to create the magic of the evenly illuminated top-lighted spaces for the north-facing studios along Cherry Street and throughout the galleries (figs. 82–83) that occupy the entirety of the second story. Yet his split criticism, scoffing at the exterior and marveling at the interior, captures the duality of the Academy that has perplexed viewers since it opened in 1876.

There was much more to the Academy design that should have interested architectural historians. Before the electric motor-driven fan, air circulation in a building was largely a matter of happenstance. Heated, lighter air rose, and cooler, denser air sank, leading to hot upper stories and damp basements. The design of field hospitals in the Civil War had led to discoveries about healthful environments, and, with the discovery of germ theory, a series of Franklin Institute lectures led to published studies on air circulation and the means to accomplish appropriate levels of ventilation. Furness utilized the temperature differential between the air in the superheated glass-roofed attic and the lower levels of the building to create a flow of air from the cooler basement to the galleries and up through the perforated steel beams that framed the skylights to the attic, where it was exhausted through the louvers of the giant industrial ventilators (see fig. 72, p. 89). These ventilators were not design affectations; rather, as in contemporary factories, these systems were conceived to make the building comfortable. Gas lights, hanging below the skylights, maintained the flow of heated air at night when the sun no longer warmed the attic.[74]

In every way, the Academy was about the new possibilities of the modern world and formed a powerful complement to the Centennial Exhibition. In its recombination of historical and global design elements, the facade became a sign of its purpose even as it divorced the architectural motifs from their context, making the building into a form of media that could communicate more than style and tradition. The Academy was a signal accomplishment of

FIG. 83 Frederick Gutekunst, albumen print showing long gallery toward the main stair, May 1876. Initially a hall of sculptures, the gallery was lighted at night by gas jets on the industrial iron rings connected to the city gas system

the mechanical age in its frank acceptance of the innovative means of construction that are evident throughout: in the exposed iron truss of the Cherry Street facade and throughout the interior; in the incorporation of the most up-to-date ventilation systems, manifested in industrial banks of louvers in the main attic and above the front galleries; in forms, materials, and details drawn from the industrial world. The Academy led the way to the future. It was not a coincidence that it was built in a city run by engineers and industrialists and that it aimed to celebrate the new American spirit.

*   *   *

History as Myth, Myth as History

THE DISCONNECTION BETWEEN the Academy's innovative design and the puzzle that it has presented to critics and historians of modern architecture results from the divorce of the standard historical narrative of modern architecture from its cultural context. When the Academy is viewed as the product of the usual interpretation of Philadelphia as socially and culturally conservative, the simplest explanation for its design has been to view it as an aberration, at odds with historical conventions devised in other places, or as lacking in reason and therefore the product of a city that either didn't care about art or was hostile to it. Such criticism, however, ignores the engineering culture that sustained the genealogy of American modernism and reached an early apogee in Centennial Philadelphia. This culture led from Frank Furness to Louis Sullivan—who took the new values west to Chicago, where he became the *lieber meister* of Frank Lloyd Wright—and set off a line of innovation that remains central to the narrative of American organic design. But Furness's office also produced the innovative designers of the Philadelphia School, led by William L. Price, who entered the office five years after Sullivan, at the time of the design and construction of the Provident Life and Trust Company.[75] Price's astonishing reinforced-concrete Atlantic City beachfront hotels (fig. 84) captured the global imagination immediately after World War I and set the stage for the so-called Art Deco style that, rather than being a European invention, was in actuality another form of Philadelphia-created contemporary design.[76]

Price was followed in the Furness office by George Howe, who arrived immediately after Furness's death. The office design process still started from the specific issues of the plan, rather than from a preconceived notion of the exterior. It was the same method that Sullivan had encountered when he worked there forty years before. Howe & Lescaze's Philadelphia Savings Fund Society (PSFS) skyscraper (fig. 85) is arguably the best American high modern building. Its differentiation of architectural volumes and forms to denote specific functions were hallmarks of the Furness method. Howe's insights, gained in the Furness office, survived into the 1950s, when he was the logical American modernist to lead the Yale School of Architecture. Howe also provides a link to Louis I. Kahn and Robert Venturi and Denise Scott Brown (b. 1931),

FIG. 84 Price & McLanahan, Traymore Hotel, Atlantic City, NJ, 1914–15 (demolished). William Price extended Furness's idea of direct expression of separate function to the hotel, which originated 1920s Art Deco FIG. 85 Howe & Lescaze, Philadelphia Savings Fund Society skyscraper, Philadelphia, 1929–32. Recalling what he had learned with Furness, Howe used highly specific volumes to represent differing functions while expressing the specifics of site in a way that became a regional standard leading on to Louis I. Kahn and Robert Venturi

who carried Furness's strategies through to the beginning of the twenty-first century. Notably, all share the architectural method and the literary sources of American organic design, the philosophy of Ralph Waldo Emerson, and the ideas about artistry of Walt Whitman (1819–1892), all of which came directly to Furness through his family, and then through him to his students. It is not a coincidence that Sullivan, Price, and Wright all quoted Emerson and Whitman, and made buildings that fit their purpose with a directness of design that befitted the industrial culture.

The standard historical narrative, which connected European modernism to the Chicago architects and then back to Boston's Henry Hobson Richardson, ignored the larger story of the industrial culture. Industrial process, which solved problems by analysis and experiment rather than by relying on precedent, formed a system in which ends were met by newly available means. Such a system was inherently disruptive to old cultural forms and to tradition. To historians seeking to reify tradition, Frank Furness's incorporation of the industrial culture into the civic architecture of Philadelphia was incomprehensible. But Furness had grown up hearing Emerson's call for Americans to represent in their culture the opportunities of their own time. His work resonated with the innovation of the coming century, and was connected to the actual process of the modern world.

First Modern

IN DECEMBER 1872, when Caleb Cope described "the new departure" of the Academy project in his address at the laying of the cornerstone, he could not have imagined how far the new building would venture from the established norms. Viewed simply as structure, the Pennsylvania Academy of the Fine Arts recapitulated the entire history of building technology in the sequence of its construction. Its masonry vaults in the basement (fig. 86), and the brick arches that carried the glass vaults of the long gallery, used vaulting techniques that reached back to Rome. But, as the building rose from the ground it began to incorporate the new technologies that we recognize as modern construction, first in the use of iron beams to span the interior rooms; then in the use of great girders to span ever-larger interior spaces; next in the use of the steel trusses of the Cherry Street facade and above the crossing of the long gallery; before finally reaching the attic, where delicate trusses carry the roof while minimizing shadows on the art below. It is a sequence that also traverses the course from masses of iron,

FIG. 86 Furness & Hewitt, basement, c. 1970s. Here, a massive flat-arched brick vault spans the masonry walls below the main stair

The masonry piers of the attic rise continuously from the massive walls in the basement, using traditional building techniques that reach back to ancient Rome

FIG. 87 Gambrill & Richardson, Trinity Episcopal Church, Boston, MA, 1872–76, with later additions. Boston's culture looks to European historical sources, as exemplified in Richardson's Back Bay church, for which Richardson bragged that "no masonry . . . is dependent on iron for support"

who referred to the machine as both "fact and symbol," incorporating the new materials and methods and giving them visual expression to ensure that the new machine model was understood.[77] Regarding intent, we have Louis Sullivan's statement that Furness made buildings "out of his head," and the future record of Furness's career as he remade and reinvented forms to meet specific purposes, as Philadelphia machine makers had made new machines. Just as important, there is engineer Fairman Rogers's statement as to the board's unwillingness to tie the design to any one system when new applications of modern techniques were so rapidly appearing. His intent to "decide upon such plans for the roof, the skylights, and the artificial lighting of the galleries as a careful consideration of these comparatively unsolved difficulties in the construction of art galleries may point out" marks the critical moment when the new possibilities of modernity replaced tradition and aimed the Academy design toward an unpredictable and dynamic future.

Instead of being like other museums in focusing on the past, on history, and on tradition, the design of the Academy resolutely looked forward. Had the board been different, then other choices would have been made; had the architects been different, other options would surely have surfaced; had they worked in other American cities, the design would have been different. But the context and the culture were industrial Philadelphia, and the Academy arose with all of its complications and new conceptions. When it was completed in the spring of 1876, architects who visited Philadelphia could see the proof of an original method that was in every way the product of the industrial culture that financed it and pushed its design directions to express the ideas of the new machine-centered culture of the Centennial city. As Coleman Sellers had remarked about machine design, "New purposes need new forms," and as Sullivan would conclude a generation later, "Form ever follows function."

Architecture as a product of a culture is at its strongest when it captures the possibilities and ideals of its time and place. Just as Henry Hobson Richardson captured Boston's reverence for history in Trinity Church (fig. 87), as Richard Morris Hunt and, later, McKim, Mead and White, expressed New York's focus on global fashion and contemporary style in the grandeur of the French-inspired Beaux-Arts, so Frank Furness grasped the potential of the age of

used in ways that a mason would find comfortable, to the countering minimalism of modern engineering that maximized strength and minimized material. The expressed structure of Renzo Piano's Pompidou Center, and more recently Piano's pyramidal glass roof for the new Harvard Art Museums building (p. 10), could have been taken directly from Frank Furness's delicate structure in the attic of the Academy.

To claim that any one building represents the beginning of modern design is, of course, absurd. As architects in mid-century New York and Philadelphia began to take advantage of the economy of cast iron for columns, and later for entire facade systems, the new began to arrive. But most of those systems paid homage to classical or Gothic details and their surface finishes, often coated with sand in the paint to provide texture, were intended to replicate stone. What sets the Academy apart is its mechanistic role, to borrow a phrase from architectural historian David Gebhard,

FIG. 88 Louis I. Kahn, Richards Medical Research Laboratories, Philadelphia, 1956–60, 1962. Kahn, raised in Philadelphia, escaped from the European International Modern as he continued to explore the representation of function that originated a century earlier in Furness's work FIG. 89 Venturi and Short, Friends Neighborhood Guild (Guild House) 1961. Venturi broke out of International Minimalism with a factual representation of the specifics of use, in a vocabulary drawn from the Guild House's setting on the edge of the industrial city

the machine and the free-thinking culture of engineering of industrial Philadelphia. The Academy marks the moment when Furness stepped away from the classical language of architecture that he had learned from Hunt to respond instead to the culture of his time and place. Its forms represent the various functions: entrance and administration in the front, the galleries stacked above the studios, with the special functions and circulation of the school at the rear. The engineer's focus on plan and logistics led to an alternate language of architectural masses that focused design on purpose. Furness had the courage to express the new values being developed in the factories and workshops of the city's industrial culture, to add the magic of light, the variety of color and texture, the symbolic use of industrial forms and materials, in order to make powerful architectural statements that still convey their message.

From the mid-nineteenth century, it has been the continuous disruptions of the industrial culture that have transformed modern life and in turn driven innovation in architectural design, spreading out from the industrialists' goals for the American Centennial Exhibition buildings and the Furness-designed banks, houses, churches, and hospitals that dotted the Centennial city and manifested the new values and possibilities. Where twentieth century European modernists relied on an intellectual construct of avant-garde "modernism" as a rejection of old orders, Philadelphia's industrialists and their architects created a different form of modern design, one that was reflected in the day-to-day life of the city and its citizens. With Furness's examples scattered across the city, evident to any young architect with eyes to see, this method extended eventually to the modern machines for laboratory work designed by Louis I. Kahn (fig. 88) and the factual Guild House (fig. 89) of Robert Venturi. In a city of engineers and with modern engines as the totem of the regional economy, Furness found both models and means to arrive at ends that we now see as modern. Wherever industrialists and their values shaped cities—whether in Philadelphia in the Centennial decade; late nineteenth-century Chicago, led by the logistics and distribution empires of the Midwest; a later Glasgow with its culture of shipbuilding and engineers; and on into the twentieth century in Prague and Berlin—architectural forms would be developed that represented the possibilities of their age. The architects who missed these opportunities now seem dated, while those few who grasped the future retain a freshness that still attracts our attention.

∗   ∗   ∗

Today

THE FIRST HALF of the twentieth century was hard on the Academy building. By 1900 the cultural origins of Frank Furness's free and direct manner had been obscured by the transition to Beaux-Arts schooling and later Euro-influenced International Modernism; as a result, the building was incomprehensible to historians and architects trained in the history-centered curriculum of the modern Beaux-Arts that had taken over the University of Pennsylvania's architecture program in the 1890s, led by Theophilus Parsons Chandler.[78] A cryptic note in the Academy minutes for early 1907 reported, "Much has been done in the past year in betterment of our building but at best the present plant is inadequate to the work attempted and the need of a new building, or additions to the present building is again emphasized." Chandler, Furness's old rival from at least the 1870s, made sketches for a sixteen-story tower at 15th and Cherry Streets that would have provided a dozen studio floors (fig. 90). Fortunately for this story, the project was never pursued.

Where the Centennial city had seen the arts as a means to improve the city's industrial production, and had created institutions in the downtown for education and display, the spatially and socially stratified city of the early twentieth century built the Philadelphia Museum of Art's palatial building at the far end of the Benjamin Franklin Parkway, where it was accessible by automobiles on roads that led to the elite suburban neighborhoods. (The Academy had been offered a new site in Paul Cret's Parkway arts district, but the project could not be funded.) The Parkway provided evidence of the ebb of the industrial culture, having been created by cutting through the zone of factories where the modern machines of William Sellers and William Bement had been invented, and where the powerful locomotives of the Baldwin Locomotive Works were built. The Parkway project caused most of these businesses to move to larger sites in the suburbs, leaving the city without an industrial identity. The city's popular identity looked backward to heritage and the American Revolution. Over the years, *The Philadelphia Story*, *Kitty Foyle*, and later *Rocky* represented the city in the national imagination.

After World War II, the Academy, blackened by the coal soot of the industrial city, was an anomaly that the new modernists scorned for its complication, its functional expressionism, and its

Emil Lukas installation, 2016, in the Academy's Morris Gallery   **107**

FIGS. 91A–B Harbeson, Hough, Livingston & Larson, alterations to front lobby, main galleries, facade, and gallery level, 1949–50. TOP At the height of International Modernism, the successors to Paul Cret, Beaux-Arts-trained professor of design at the University of Pennsylvania, created a modern glass and stainless steel entryway in place of Furness's massive iron gates and wood vestibule (since largely restored) BOTTOM The exuberant steel and iron columns of the long gallery were encased in drywall boxes and the walls were painted a uniform white

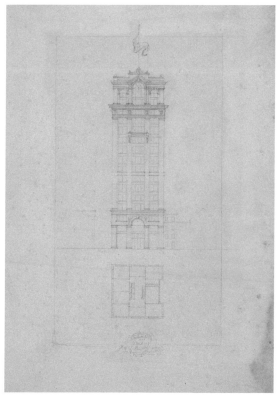

FIG. 90 Theophilus Parsons Chandler, 1907. A board member and Furness rival, Chandler proposed a slender tower on Cherry Street to house the studios and academic offices of the growing institution

historical details, missing its role in laying the foundations for the style of architecture that they practiced. In the early 1950s, the firm of Harbeson, Hough, Livingston & Larson was hired to freshen the building's interior, creating one of the first modern gallery spaces in the city. The Victorian doors and iron gates at the Broad Street front were scrapped; the huge industrial ventilators and roofs that capped the north and south wings were no longer in use and were removed; the wood entrance vestibule was demolished and replaced with a stainless steel and glass enclosure (fig. 91A); and the gallery walls were painted international modern white. Institutional management muted the interior: the brilliant hues of the stair hall tiles were painted battleship grey and the bronze balustrade and walnut railings of the stairs were painted black. In the galleries, the pipe columns and the cast decorative heads were encased in minimalist plasterboard boxes (fig. 91B).

FIG. 92 Thomas Armstrong, academy director 1971–73, c. 1973

FIG. 93 Hyman Myers, restoration architect, 1974, shows the rediscovered triangular vestibule between the long gallery and side galleries that had been sealed off in the 1950s renovations

FIG. 94 Hyman Myers receives the Furness Prize for his work as the restoration architect from academy director Richard Boyle, 1976

Ironically, a decade earlier, John Harbeson (1888–1986), the head of the architectural firm altering the building, had written a laudatory article on "Philadelphia's Victorian Architecture, 1860–1890," with particular praise for Furness as

> the one who was responsible for the best architecture of the period—the one whose work had the most influence on the architecture of today. It is true that he did some of the worst also, for his effort varies much in quality; but it was never commonplace, it was always daring and it is this daring that was at times disastrous in taste. Furness' work is original, independent in conception, and in it may be found the germs of much contemporary architectural thought.[79]

Noting Furness's industrial inventions and describing the logic and clarity of his planning, particularly for the still-standing Broad Street Station, Harbeson continued:

> But it is the plan that is remarkable here, for it is very much the type of composition attempted today by architects of what is called the "International School." It has "flowing space"; there is no symmetry, no use of architectural "axes." The planning is purely functional—that is to say, dictated by use; and it proved excellent for railroad use even in the busy twenties. It cared for the arrival

> and the departure of passengers without the one interfering with the other, and for all the details of tickets and baggage and hurried meals.[80]

By the 1970s, in the midst of the major reevaluation of the principles and sources of modern design exemplified in the work of the Philadelphia School led by Louis I. Kahn, with Robert Venturi's *Complexity and Contradiction in Architecture* as a theory, and *Learning from Las Vegas* by Denise Scott Brown, Robert Venturi, and Steve Izenour (1941–2001) as an example of learning from contemporary life, Furness came into focus as a historical source for the Philadelphia School. After the board first proposed to sell the historic Academy to move the collection to Independence Mall, advocates for Furness and his first masterpiece called for the restoration of the building as a part of the city's celebration of the nation's Bicentennial. Academy director Thomas Armstrong (1932–2011; fig. 92) and Furness advocate and architect Hyman Myers (b. 1941; figs. 93–94), who, ironically, was the same age that Furness had been when the building was initially constructed, directed the refurbishment. The update restored the exterior masonry to its original brilliance, removing the stucco panels that covered the exterior steel truss on the Cherry Street facade and revealing the muscular iron for the first time since it was covered in the early twentieth century; recreating the iron grills and doors and the entrance vestibule; repainting and gilding the tiles of the stair hall; removing the drywall covers of the iron columns; and returning the building to its original vibrancy. Once again, it was possible to see Furness, in Harbeson's phrase, as "the ablest of these experimenters, these pioneers."

Louis Sullivan's description of the Bloomfield Moore house that drew him to the Furness office as "like a flower by the roadside," and "something fresh and fair . . . a human note, as though someone were talking," applies also to the Pennsylvania Academy of the Fine Arts. Unlike the repetitive manner of the later Beaux-Arts classicism that relied on classical formulations and manufactured columns and moldings from giant stone yards in Indiana, Furness's Academy and his later works were "daring" and "independent in conception," startlingly original and not cheapened by replication.[81] Unlike the modern skyscraper icons of 1950s New York City that were knocked off in vast numbers, to the point that they became boring, Furness's buildings were so specific to purpose that they were rarely copied. These qualities still draw our eyes to the Academy, which, even in its diminished condition—caused by the removal of the great ventilators from its front facade and having been surrounded by far larger buildings—demands attention. In it are anticipated the heroic representationalism of Kahn, the sometimes comic heraldry of Venturi, the free sculpturalism of Frank Gehry, and the iconoclastic adventurism of Rem Koolhaas. In so many ways, Frank Furness's Pennsylvania Academy of the Fine Arts was the first civic modern building, one that began the lines of creation that have led to the truly innovative architecture of our time.

Academy Board of Directors in the Chestnut Street building, after the collection was removed, just before it was sold, 1870. Left to right: Joseph Harrison Jr., A. M. Stevenson, James L. Claghorn, Henry G. Morris, Caleb Cope, John Sartain, and William Struthers

APPENDIX THE SUBSCRIPTION LIST

The list of subscribers, with its supplement, is a remarkable one that demonstrates the new cultural elite of the industrial city. Here, the new industrialists are indentified "+" and the old mercantile culture "$." The subscriptions include twenty-five payments of $10,000, fifteen of $5,000, fourteen of $2,500, twelve of $2,000, and eighty-six of $1,000, in the order named, as follows:

$10,000 donors: Joseph Harrison Jr.,+ Alfred D. Jessup,+ J. Gillingham Fell,+ Fairman Rogers,+ Henry C. Gibson,$ William Sellers & Co.,+ Matthew Baird,+ A. Whitney & Sons,+ William B. Bement,+ Andrew M. Moore,+ Thomas A. Scott,+ Clement Biddle,$ Thomas Dolan,+ Henry G. Morris,+ J. Edgar Thomson,+ Henry H. Houston,+ William Massey,+ Morris, Tasker & Co.,+ McKean & Borie,$ Powers & Weightman,+ Edwin N. Benson,$ David S. Brown,$ Friend of the Institute, George S. Pepper,$ Burnham, Parry, Williams & Co.+

$5,000: William J. Horstmann,+ French, Richards & Co.,+ Alexander Brown,$ A. Campbell, Lewis Audenried,+ John Dobson,+ E. W. Clark & Co.,$ S. &. W. Welsh,+ Fairman Rogers,+ Henry C. Gibson,$ Clarence H. Clark,$ W. E. Garrett & Sons, William T. Carter, Thomas A. Scott,$ George F. T. Reed

$2,500: Jacob Riegel & Co., Thackara, Buck & Co., J. E. Kingsley, Elliott, Collins & Co., Coffin & Altemus, J. E. Caldwell & Co., Shortridge, Borden & Co. John Bohlen, Joseph Singerly, James L. Claghorn, William Sellers & Co.,+ Alexander Brown, George F. T. Reed, Charles F. Haseltine, Anthony J. Drexel$

$2,000: Francis A. Drexel,$ William H. Kemble,$ Baeder, Adamson & Co., Caleb Cope,$ Theodore Cuyler,$ George W. Hill, Estate of Henry Seybert, James S. Martin, Daniel Haddock Jr., Charles H. Rogers, Charles E. Claghorn, George W. Fales, Alfred G. Baker, P. Jenks Smith, Samuel Baugh

NOTES

1 The description of a house as "a machine for living" by Charles-Édouard Jeanneret-Gris (Le Corbusier) in *Vers une architecture* (1923), translated as *Towards a New Architecture* (1927), is the best-known use of the machine metaphor for architecture freed from history. See also David Gebhard, "The Moderne in the U.S.," *Architectural Association Quarterly*, 2, no. 3 (July 1970): pp. 4–20, which opens with Frank Lloyd Wright's 1901 paean to the machine, "the engine, the motor, and the battleship, the work of art of the century," from Edgar Kauffman and Ben Raeburn, eds., *Frank Lloyd Wright: Writings and Buildings* (New York: Meridian, 1960), p. 59. Working from the standard Euro-historical narrative, Gebhard missed the links between Wright and Furness and the Philadelphia industrial culture.

2 Instead of being carved or drilled, with the work tool controlled by the hand of a craftsman, much of the ornament of the stonework of the Academy was blasted using grit propelled by air. A rubber pattern protected the unworked zone, eliminating any aspect of handwork to create a perfectly repetitive design. This was but one of many instances in which the new processes of the machine age were applied to making the building—from the machine-made bricks and large sheets of glass of the skylights, to the iron trusses of the north facade, and the structure of the interior. See n. 57.

3 The dimensions of modernity are described by Anthony Giddens in *Modernity and Self-Identity: Self and Society in the Late Modern Age* (Stanford, CA: Stanford University Press, 1991).

4 For the best account of Peale's assemblage of art and curios, see David Rodney Brigham, *A World in Miniature: Charles Willson Peale's Philadelphia Museum and its Audience, 1786–1827* (University of Pennsylvania PhD dissertation, 1992). Peale's aim was to democratize and promote useful knowledge, anticipating David Hackett Fischer's differentiation of Philadelphia's Quaker-led culture from Boston's Congregational culture. See Fischer, *Albion's Seed: Four British Folkways in America* (New York: Oxford University Press, 1989).

5 Paul Semonin, *American Monster: How the Nation's First Prehistoric Creature Became a Symbol of National Identity* (New York: NYU Press, 2000).

6 "Correspondence," *American Architect and Building News*, 2, no. 60 (February 17, 1877): p. 58.

7 Thomas Carlyle, "Signs of the Times," *Edinburgh Review* 98 (1829), reprinted, *The Complete Works of Thomas Carlyle*, vol. 1. (New York: P. F. Collier & Sons, 1901), pp. 462–87. Carlyle proclaimed the "mechanical age" and its conflict with tradition.

8 An innovative educational system introduced by British Quaker Joseph Lancaster (1778–1838). Lancaster visited Philadelphia in 1818 to train teachers to implement his system in a model school. www.britannica.com/biography /Joseph-Lancaster

9 For the early athenaeum, see Josiah Quincy, *History of the Boston Athenaeum with Biographical Notices of its Deceased Founders* (Cambridge: Metcalf and Company, 1851), pp. 7; 42–43. The annual membership fee in 1807 was $10, two weeks' pay at the time, which had risen by the 1820s to three payments totaling $300, the amount of a year's wage for a workman. Philadelphia's Athenaeum was founded eight years later in 1815; its Historical Society was formed in the fall of 1824. See Lee Schreiber, "Bluebloods and Local Societies: A Philadelphia Microcosm," *Pennsylvania History*, 48, no. 3 (July 1981): pp. 251–66. William H. Wahl, *The Franklin Institute, 1824–1894* (Philadelphia: the Institute, 1895), particularly the introduction which paraphrases Wahl's talk at the fiftieth anniversary in 1874. Membership dues of $6 per year brought a subscription to the monthly *Journal of the Franklin Institute*, but meetings were open to the public and the library was free to all.

10 Bruce Sinclair, "At the Turn of a Screw: William Sellers, the Franklin Institute and a Standard American Screw," *Technology and Culture*, 10, no. 1 (January 1969): pp. 20–34.

11 For an overview of the early boards of the Academy and other "learned societies" of Philadelphia, see Schreiber, "Bluebloods and Local Societies," pp. 251–66.

12 Caleb Cope, "Address," *Exercises at the Laying of the Cornerstone of the New Building for the Pennsylvania Academy of the Fine Arts December 7, 1872* (Philadelphia: Collins Printer, 1872), pp. 6–8. The comparison with other galleries marks the ongoing competition between cities, with the prospective Academy exceeding the size of Washington, DC's, Corcoran Gallery and New York's National Academy of Design.

13 A contemporary biography of Claghorn can be found in Benjamin Comegys, "James Lawrence Claghorn," *Advice to Young Boys and Men* (Philadelphia: Gebbie & Co. 1890), pp. 129–42.

14 Richard Arthington Gilpin was variously listed as engineer and architect. A graduate of the University of Pennsylvania in 1830, he added a Master's degree in 1833. In 1836 he proposed a vehicular tunnel under the Schuylkill; he was a competitor for the Philadelphia Athenaeum (awarded to John Notman); and immediately after the Academy building he was engaged at the United States Naval Academy in Annapolis. Anna Wharton Smith, *Genealogy of the Fisher Family: 1682–1896* (Philadelphia, 1896), p. 62.

15 John Sartain, *Reminiscences of a Very Old Man* (New York: D. Appleton Company, 1899), pp. 250–51. Sartain's autobiography is untrustworthy on numerous points, including the name of the architect of the second Academy building, whom he lists as John Haviland instead of Richard Gilpin, but it provides an overview of his activities in Philadelphia after his arrival in 1830. He became a board member in 1855 and continued in that role until 1877. His narrative of his Academy work begins p. 155 ff. The best modern account of Sartain is Katharine Martinez and Page Talbott, eds., *Philadelphia's Cultural Landscape: The Sartain Family Legacy* (Philadelphia: Temple University Press, 2000).

16 Whitney's interests in the arts led him to a board position at the Academy and later as a lender to New York's Metropolitan Museum of Art. See Linda S. Ferber, *Tokens of a Friendship: Miniature Watercolors by William Trost Richards* (New York: Metropolitan Museum of Art, 1982; New Haven: Yale University Press, 2013, in association with the Academy exhibition), p. 21 ff.

17 Pennsylvania Academy of the Fine Arts (PAFA) Archives, Board of Trustees Minutes 1858–1876 (November 14, 1864), pp. 185–86; (January 16, 1865), p. 193.

18 PAFA Archives, Board of Trustees Minutes (August 29, 1867), pp. 236–37.

19 In their proximity, there may have been the intent to create the type of agglomeration of institutions, museums, and collections that had been proposed in the previous decade for South Kensington, London. See Bruce Robertson, "The South Kensington Museum in context: an alternative history," *Museum and Society*, 2, no. 1 (March 2004): pp. 1–14. The role of the museum for education across all dimensions of culture is evident in Robertson's aside. "As late as 1866, one could go to the South Kensington Museum and see salmon and trout hatch, on the way to look at Turner's pictures, having just perused the latest medieval acquisitions," p. 6. Similar juxtapositions would have been possible had

Center Square been adopted as Philadelphia's museum complex.

20 PAFA Archives, Board of Trustees Minutes (December 24, 1870).

21 Joseph Harrison Jr., *The Iron Worker and King Solomon together with a memoir and an appendix* (Philadelphia: J. B. Lippincott & Co. 1868).

22 Coleman Sellers, "An Obituary Notice of Mr. Joseph Harrison, Jr." *The Proceedings of the American Philosophical Society,* 14, no. 94 (February 1875): pp. 347–55. Unfortunately, when the house was demolished in the 1920s no record was made of these elements. Some of the "ingenious devices" may be visible on the garden facade where a conservatory and a glazed sunroom were constructed of cast iron.

23 PAFA Archives, Board of Trustees Minutes (June 12, 1871), p. 368.

24 The garage and its gasoline tanks caused significant alterations to the exterior of the Academy in the early twentieth century in order to fireproof the building. This resulted in covering and fireproofing the exposed steel truss of the Cherry Street facade, and replacing all the wood window frames of the exterior with steel. PAFA Archives, Broad and Cherry Renovations and Repairs Box (BCRR), 1910–1916 Invoices Folder, Trask to Appleton & Burrell, July 24, 1911; invoice Appleton & Burrell, September 19, 1911. See also *Annual Report,* 1912. The garage was the focus of exterior repairs in 1913, BCRR, 1877–1899 folder, letter from Theophilus Parsons Chandler (1845–1928) to Academy recommending covering of exterior steel truss, June 21, 1913. That work was accomplished, BCRR, 1910–1916 invoices folder, James T. Allen & Son, for metal lath and plaster over the truss, October 4, 1913.

25 This idea persisted from the eighteenth century differentiation between the spatial location of "proper" Philadelphians and their institutions south of Market and that of Germans and other nationalities to the north. It was still alive in popular fiction into the early twentieth century. See Katharine Bingham, *The Philadelphians* (Boston: L. C. Page & Co., 1903), pp. 13–15, especially, "In Philadelphia to live uptown is to be unknown by the kind of people whom you are accustomed to. Fashionable society—those whom you would call the 'nice people'—all live in a very small section of the city, the oldest part, and nothing would induce them to set foot in any part north of Market Street, much less live there."

26 PAFA Archives, Board of Trustees Minutes (December 24, 1870), p. 343, reported that Fairman Rogers had replaced Harrison on the board.

27 Gideon Fairman was born in Newtown, Connecticut, and moved to Philadelphia in 1810. First Unitarian Church Records 1796–1979, Historic Pennsylvania Church and Town Records, Historical Society of Pennsylvania, microfilm reel 847. See Henry Simpson, *The Lives of Eminent Philadelphians, Now Deceased* (Philadelphia: William Brotherhood, 1859), pp. 357–58.

28 Edgar Fahs Smith, "Biographical Memoir of Fairman Rogers—1833–1900," read before the National Academy of Sciences, November 22, 1906, *Biographical Memoirs of the National Academy of Sciences,* 6 (1909): pp. 93–107. While Rogers was heading the Academy's building committee, he was also leading the group that authored *History of the First Troop Philadelphia City Cavalry 1774, November 17, 1874* (Printed for the Troop, Hallowell & Co., 1875). Many of the troopers became Furness clients and several served in the Sixth Pennsylvania Cavalry with Furness. For Rogers's roles in the Institute, see *Journal of the Franklin Institute,* 47, no. 6 (June 1864): p. 422.

29 Martinez, ed., *Philadelphia's Cultural Landscape: The Sartain Family*, p. 12.

30 John Woolf Jordan, *Colonial Families of Philadelphia,* 2 (New York: Lewis Publishing Company, 1911), pp. 541–45.

31 "Obituary, Henry G. Morris," *Journal of the American Society of Mechanical Engineers*, 37 (April 1915): p. 244.

32 Gibson's collection is typical of his day, with his tastes running to Rosa Bonheur and Thomas Couture. See Charles Henry Hart, "The Public and Private Collections of the United States: The Collection of Mr. Henry C. Gibson, Philadelphia," *The American Art Review* 1 (April 1880), pp. 231–35; and part 2 (May 1880), pp. 293–99. That article concludes with remarks on Gustav Courbet, who had painted the *Great Oak-Tree of Ornans* that was owned by Gibson. "Courbet, the partisan of the Commune, the destroyer of the Vendome column, who prided himself upon being the head of the realistic school in France, and who preferred ugliness to beauty, because his nature was coarse and unrefined and soulless."

33 Various board members were suggested for the building committee, including William Sellers, the premier machine tool maker of his day, who was then devoting much of his time to the new campus of the University of Pennsylvania; Clarence Clark, a financier and banker with a strong connection to the Philadelphia Unitarian congregation led by William Henry Furness; Charles Macalister, financier and insurance executive; Adolph Borie, another financier and close friend of President Ulysses S. Grant; Alfred Dupont Jessup, paper manufacturer and partner of Bloomfield Moore, afterwards a client of Furness & Hewitt; George Whitney, art collector and manufacturer of iron railroad wheels. All declined for various reasons. Most were members of the Union League, but many were advanced in age and not looking for new tasks or, in the case of Sellers, adding a new task to his work for the Centennial and the University board.

34 PAFA Catalogued Building Construction Box, 1871–2 folder: June 19, 1871: letter to John Sartain from John Windrim (son of James H.) requesting more specifications for the competition.

35 The house on Broad Street that Sloan designed for Morris is listed in Harold N. Cooledge, *Samuel Sloan: Architect of Philadelphia, 1815–1884* (Philadelphia: University of Pennsylvania Press, 1986); for Hutton's biography see Elizabeth Biddle Yarnall, *Addison Hutton: Quaker Architect, 1834–1916* (Philadelphia: Art Alliance Press, 1974). Windrim has yet to receive a thorough publication; see Sandra Tatman, "James Hamilton Windrim, 1840–1919," Philadelphia Architects and Buildings, www.philadelphiabuildings.org/pab/app/ar_display.cfm/21564. Sims has been treated by Leslie Beller, "The Diary of Henry A. Sims," MA thesis, University of Pennsylvania, 1974, and more recently by Michael J. Lewis, "The Architectural Library of Henry A. Sims," in *American Architects and their Books, 1840–1915*, eds. Kenneth Hafertepe and James F. O'Gorman (Amherst: University of Massachusetts Press, 2007), pp. 173–93. Richards also awaits a biographer. His University of Pennsylvania work is treated by George E. Thomas, "Thomas Webb Richards," and in the chapter "Mining . . . and Other Kindred Subjects," Ann Strong and George E. Thomas, *The Book of the School: A Century of the Graduate School of Fine Arts* (Philadelphia: Graduate School of Fine Arts, 1990), pp. 3–12.

36 The American Academy of Music competition before the Civil War had called for a marble facade with an alternate of brick. Philadelphians referred to the brick Academy of Music as looking like a city market, i.e. a utilitarian structure; always aware of New York, they also would have known of the marble facade of New York's recently completed National Academy of Design by Peter B. Wight (1838–1925). None of the first group of drawings remains, but the perspective published in *Lippincott's Magazine* shows the winning scheme, which was largely as built in the massing, though not in the details.

37 John Fraser to John Sartain, October 5, 1871, PAFA Furness Building files.

38 John Sartain to Thomas W. Richards, November 2, 1871, Thomas W. Richards Papers, University of Pennsylvania Archives. Sartain was right about funding. Rogers gave $5,000 to the project, roughly 1 percent of the estimated construction cost.

39 This source was pointed out to the author by Michael J. Lewis.

40 PAFA Archives, Board of Trustees Minutes (November 13, 1871), pp. 370–74.

41 "The New Academy of Fine Arts," *Philadelphia Inquirer*, November 16, 1871, p. 2: "The different plans for the new building have been examined by the Board of Directors of the Academy of Fine Arts and they find them unsatisfactory in regard to elevation and the detail of the facade. Messrs. Hewitt & Furness have been chosen as architects, under the direction of the Board. The interior has already been designed and the plans have been published. The work on the new Academy will be commenced early in the spring."

42 PAFA Archives, Board of Trustees Minutes (December 11, 1871), p. 376.

43 Robert Venturi, *Complexity and Contradiction in Modern Architecture* (New York: Museum of Modern Art, 1966), p. 32.

44 Louis Sullivan, *Autobiography of an Idea* (1924; reprint New York: Dover Publishing Co, 1956), pp. 190–96. Beginning in 1922, the autobiography was published serially in the *Journal of the American Institute of Architects.*

45 Sullivan, *Autobigraphy of an Idea*, p. 193.

46 The planning for the cornerstone laying ceremony is described in PAFA Minutes 1858–1876, 1872, pp. 417–19. "Address of Fairman Rogers" for the laying of the cornerstone, *Exercises at the Laying of the Cornerstone of the New Building of the Pennsylvania Academy of the Fine Arts December 7 1872* (Philadelphia: Collins Printer, 1872), pp. 12–13.

47 Hammered glass was made by pouring molten glass on a beaten metal plate that produced a texture that diffused light. Sizes available in Philadelphia were listed in *Sloan's Architectural Review and Builders' Journal* (Nov. 1868): p. 321. Flooring glass in 1¼ inch plate was available in sheets up to 24 × 36 inches; hammered glass for skylighting in ½ inch plate was available in sizes up to 30 × 120 inches. Committee decision, PAFA Building Committee Minutes, February 12, 1873.

48 H[orace] H[oward] F[urness], *F. R. 1833–1900* (Philadelphia, 1903), p. 13. Frank Furness's brother Horace, in his obituary essay for his brother-in-law Fairman Rogers, noted his contributions to the Academy design: "In its internal design and arrangement, much that is admirable and best is owing to his careful and earnest thought."

49 Ralph Waldo Emerson, "The American Scholar," *The Complete Writings of Ralph Waldo Emerson* (1875; reprint New York: William Wise, 1929), p. 111 ff. An unfinished portrait of Emerson by the Reverend Dr. Furness's son William is in the PAFA collection (see p. 16).

50 Emerson, "Success," *Complete Writings* (1904), vol 7, pp. 281–312.

51 Emerson, "The Young American," *Complete Writings*, p. 111.

52 William Henry Furness, "The Architect an Artist," lecture given November 9, 1870, to the American Institute of Architects, published, *The Penn Monthly, 2*, no. 6 (June 1871), pp. 295–308.

53 Ibid.

54 John Ruskin, *Lectures on Architecture and Painting Delivered Edinburgh in November 1853* (New York: John Wiley & Sons, 1884), pp. 53–54.

55 There is a consistent literature on this topic, beginning with Edwin T. Freedley, *Manufactures of Philadelphia* (Philadelphia: Edward Young, 1858), throughout, but especially pp. 131–35, 314–16, and 328. The topic was also picked up by the Franklin Institute, "Editorial: American Machinery Abroad," *Journal of the Franklin Institute*, 66, no. 5 (November 1873): pp. 349–56. This editorial made the economic argument that high wages and material costs caused Americans to look for ever-more efficient systems to keep production costs in line with other nations, accounting for the degree of American mechanization. William Sellers's machines were praised for the same values in the Centennial Judges' Reports: Francis A. Walker, ed., *United States Centennial Commission, International Exhibition 1876, 7* Reports and Awards Groups 21–27, "Group 21: Machine Tools for Metal, Wood and Stone" (Washington, DC, 1880), pp. 14–18. These Philadelphia-initiated design theories have been confused with the larger American culture, missing the particular local character of these ideas. See John Kouwenhoven, *Made in America: The Arts in Modern Civilization* (Garden City, New York: Doubleday and Company, 1949), p. 106. See especially the chapter "The Practical and the Aesthetic," pp. 96–117.

56 Coleman Sellers, quoted in Wahl, *The Franklin Institute, 1824–1894*, pp. 44–45. The idea that architecture was additive to structure comes from Ruskin.

57 Louis Sullivan, "The Tall Office Building Artistically Considered," *Lippincott's Magazine,* 57 (March, 1896), pp. 403–9. Sullivan tellingly begins with the idea of the "evolution and integration of social conditions," "if we follow our natural instincts without thought of books, rules, precedents, or any such educational impedimenta to a spontaneous and 'sensible' result, we will in the following manner design the exterior of our tall office building." "All things in nature have a shape, that is to say, a form, an outward semblance, that tells us what they are, that distinguishes them from ourselves and from each other." *Lippincott's Magazine*, a Philadelphia publication, had printed Furness's "Hints to Designers," May 1878 (vol. 21), pp. 612–14.

58 The glass roofed and walled photographic studio of Parisian photographer Charles Reutlinger is illustrated in the *Philadelphia Photographer*, 6, no. 64 (April 1869), p. 115. The studio is described in 6, no. 61 (January 1869), pp. 30–31. https://archive.org/stream /philadelphiaphot1869phil#page/114 /mode/2up. Photography brought together the sciences and the arts, a conjunction that was nowhere more in evidence than in the Photographic Society of Philadelphia. The society's leaders included Fairman Rogers, Coleman Sellers, and city engineer Frederick Graff. See John C. Browne, "History of the Photographic Society of Philadelphia, A Paper Read before the Society, December 3, 1883." See also Walter Zimmerman, "The Oldest American Photographic Society," *American Photography, 2*, no. 8 (August 1908), pp. 486–92. It lists Frederick Gutekunst as another of the founding members. Rogers and Eakins may well have known each other prior to the latter's role as instructor in drawing at the Academy in the late 1870s, as both were deeply involved in photography. By the 1860s, Rogers had designed a rotating shutter mechanism that permitted multiple images on the same glass plate and could capture and stop movement, which he demonstrated at the Photographic Society of Philadelphia in 1871. Accounts of early meetings in February and May 1863 provide the flavor of scientific inquiry. See "The Photographic Society of Philadelphia," *The British Journal of Photography,* 9 (February 16, 1863, and May 1, 1863), pp. 82, 83, 195. While critics sneered that Eakins was a "scientist not an artist," his work in photography made significant advances. In 1883, Eakins showed the members his invention of a drop shutter with speeds which he demonstrated between 1/100 to 1/1500th second. "Photography in Philadelphia," *Photographer,* 13, no. 156 (December 1883), pp. 654–57. Eakins's invention is described on p. 657. Rogers's rotating shutter to stop action was developed long before Eadweard Muybridge's better-known, but less sophisticated, wires and multiple cameras used for his *Animal Locomotion* photographs under

the auspices of Leland Stanford on the west coast. Nonetheless, when Stanford withdrew support, it would be Rogers who offered facilities at the University of Pennsylvania, on whose board he also sat, to enable Muybridge to continue his work.

59 G. F. Barker, "Sand Blast," *Johnson's New Universal Cyclopaedia,* vol. 4 (New York: Alvin J. Johnson & Son, 1878), p. 64.

60 Sullivan, *Autobiography of an Idea,* p. 195. Note that although an autobiography, the book was written in the third person.

61 PAFA Archives, Board of Trustees Minutes (December 8, 1873), pp. 443–4.

62 PAFA Archives, Catalogued Building Construction, Atkinson & Myhlertz, to John Sartain, April 10, 1874.

63 PAFA Archives, Catalogued Building Construction Box, Letter, Furness & Hewitt to Fairman Rogers, December 15, 1873. They requested $3,000 because of the additional work and time for the construction.

64 PAFA Archives, Building Committee Minutes, April 15, 1874, and June 8, 1874.

65 Morris, Tasker & Co. *Illustrated Catalogue*: *Pascal Iron Works, Philadelphia* (1875). https://archive.org/stream/IllustratedCatalogue PascalIronWorks/CCA15334#page/n3/mode/2up

66 PAFA Archives, Board of Trustees Minutes (May 1, 1875), pp. 470–71.

67 This request was made by Charles Wheeler, president of Morris, Wheeler, & Co., when he was approached for funds for Bryn Mawr's Protestant Episcopal Church of the Redeemer. Maria Thompson pointed out this important requirement. Vestry of the Church of the Redeemer, Minutes, The Committee on Plans of the Vestry of the Church of the Redeemer, Aug. 8, 1879, archives of the Church of the Redeemer, Bryn Mawr, Pennsylvania.

68 http://ansp.pastperfect-online.com/40100cgi/mweb.exe?request=kcyword;keyword=collection%20049;dtype=d

69 Ironically, Europeans were quick to grasp the innovations of the Philadelphia machinery designs, but none saw the parallel to the new buildings of the Centennial, particularly the Academy.

70 "Centennial Exposition Memoranda," *Potters American Monthly*, 7, no. 58 (October 1876), p. 316.

71 Nikolaus Pevsner, in *A History of Building Types* (Princeton University Press, 1976), p. 131. Pevsner attended the Society of Architectural Historians conference in Philadelphia in mid-May 1976 and visited the newly reopened building.

72 The ventilating cupola of the Academy of Music is an antecedent to the Academy of the Fine Arts's giant ventilators, but it was classical in form instead of the direct industrial shape that Furness used. Further, because of its placement in the center of its roof, it was invisible from the street. For the best contemporary discussion of the new building, see "Academy of the Fine Arts, Philadelphia," *Art Journal,* n.s. 2 (New York, 1876): p. 202.

73 Ibid.

74 We have no direct description of the mechanical systems of the Academy, other than the drawings and the surviving chases and ventilator elements in the building. Contemporary interest in the subject in Philadelphia is evident in the seven lectures given between 1866 and 1868 at the Franklin Institute by Louis W. Leeds. These were published as *A Treatise on Ventilation* (New York: John Wiley & Son, 1868); the illustrations in Leeds's book have long been used to illustrate Victorian ventilation design. See also Robert Ritchie, *A Treatise on Ventilation: Natural and Artificial* (London: Lockwood & Co., 1862). Furness's interest in the subject can be gauged from the slightly later Jefferson Hospital, whose mechanical systems were extensively discussed by H. O., "The Jefferson Medical College Hospital," *The Boston Medical and Surgical Journal*, 96, no. 8 (February 1877): pp. 236–41. It mentions the architects as Furness & Hewitt, but places the design at the hands of Furness. "The style of architecture may be termed eclectic, not being modeled after any one school. Mr. Furness has evidently depended on his unfailing originality, and as usual has given universal satisfaction." The article describes the mechanical and ventilating systems in detail and suggests parallels to the original Academy systems.

75 Price's father, James Price, headed the insurance department and saw that two of his sons, Francis (afterwards Frank) and William, were placed in the Furness office. A receipt book from the bank that recorded work completed and payments to the office, signed by Furness and, toward the end of the construction, by Frank Price, has been acquired by the Architectural Archives of the University of Pennsylvania.

76 George E. Thomas, *William L. Price: From Arts and Crafts to Modern Design* (New York: Princeton Architectural Press, 2000), especially pp. 236–51.

77 Gebhard, "The Moderne in the U.S.," p. 4.

78 See Strong and Thomas, *The Book of the School, 100 Years*, especially "The Laird Years: A Group Enthusiasm," pp. 23–93.

79 John Harbeson, "Philadelphia's Victorian Architecture, 1860–1890," *Pennsylvania Magazine of History and Biography*, 67, no. 3 (July 1943): pp. 254–71. The 1876 photograph of the Academy is published with the article, p. 267.

80 Harbeson, p. 269.

81 Harbeson, p. 266.

The industrial iron beams and steel columns of the second story frame the installation *Melt/Carve/ Forge: Embodied Sculptures by Cassils*, 2016–17

The light in the building is ever variable, changing the way that art is seen depending on the time of day, the season, and the weather. *Alyson Shotz: Plane Weave*, 2016

TOP The truss of the Cherry Street elevation makes possible the strip window of the Morris Gallery, emphasizing the essential modernity of the concept BOTTOM *Emil Lukas*, 2016 OPPOSITE *Melt/Carve/Forge: Embodied Sculptures by Cassils*, 2016–17

The earliest photographs of the stair hall show lamps in the form of clusters of storks standing back-to-back, with an oil reservoir between their necks; those were quickly gone, replaced by these lamps, based on sketches in the Furness notebooks

Chronology

ASSEMBLED BY ISAAC KORNBLATT-STIER

ABBREVIATIONS:

BM = board minutes

BCM = building committee minutes

CBC = catalogued building construction box

FBA = Furness building articles box

F&H = Furness & Hewitt

Texts are summarized with particular information in quotes.

FORMAT: DATE, DESCRIPTION, SOURCE IN ARCHIVES.

JULY 25, 1869 The existing Academy building is sold for $140,000, including the ground. There is a call to "let a new and fairer Academy arise in a desirable locality, under new promise, and with new means." *Sunday [Philadelphia] Times,* Philadelphia (PR box including year 1869)

MAY 8, 1870 "Sunday . . . an extraordinary storm of hail occurred and lasted probably from fifteen to twenty minutes. In that time it utterly destroyed all the skylights of the academy galleries. . . . The large skylight over the North gallery was composed of thick hammered glass, yet, of all this, but one pane remained unbroken." Academy committee minutes (misc. board minutes box)

NOVEMBER 15, 1870 The board agrees to purchase from James Steele "ground and the buildings thereon erected situated at the South West corner of Broad and Cherry Streets, containing One hundred feet on the former street, and extending back two hundred and sixty feet on the latter street, for the price or sum of ninety five thousand dollars lawful money to be paid." FBA Force report appendix doc.

DEC 24, 1870 The purchase is confirmed, and the board resolves to fund the erection of the new Academy by "subscriptions made payable in installments of one, two and three years—optional however with the subscribers." BM1858–76, p. 343

FEBRUARY 11, 1871 The board issues an invitation to attend a preliminary building planning meeting on the 27th at the Continental Hotel; attendees: W. Charles Macalister ("called to the chair"), Caleb Cope, Claghorn, Whitney, Gibson, Fairman Rogers, Chas. H. Rogers, Morris, Bement, D. Lewis, John Haseltine, M. Baird, Peter Rothermel, Haddock,

Sartain; Joseph Harrison Jr. is still listed as being a board member. Figure I-001. BCM

FEBRUARY 27, 1871 Caleb Cope tells the board "that in the adoption of a plan for the arrangement of rooms for study of cast from the antique, lecture, library, life class, and other accommodations for the academy on the ground floor, with picture galleries over, lit by skylights, he believed that it was not necessary to cover the whole ground with building at the present time, but suggested that the design would be arranged that the building could be extended at a future day without marring the unity of the plan."

Cope says that he has requested John Sartain to "draw up a plan for the arrangement of rooms and galleries adapted to the wants of the institution, which had been accordingly done and he submitted the drawing of both floors, which would serve the purpose of a starting point for future development. The building was made to extend only so far west as was necessary to place the window lighting the life class room opposite the small street running north from Cherry St. as it was important to the have the pure light of the sky in that apartment." BCM: Continental Hotel

APRIL 10, 1871 A lengthy letter from Cope indicates that the Academy's current bad finances are the fault of the departure from the board of Joseph Harrison Jr.; contrary to Harrison's recommendation, Cope argued that the new Academy should not be built in a park, and the schools should be suspended until finances get better—a suggestion that is voted on and approved. BM1858–76, pp. 354–60

SIDE ONE UNDATED (LIKELY BETWEEN JUNE 12 AND 19), SIDE TWO JUNE 19 "Present Mr. Sartain, Gibson, Claghorn, Rogers; Mr. Sartain Chairman - Mr. Rogers Secretary." The board resolves that "Architects be invited to enter into an open competition for designs for a new building for the Academy of Fine Arts. . . . On motion of Mr. Gibson it was resolved that Five Hundred Dollars be paid to the successful competitor, three hundred to the second and two hundred to the third. . . . On motion of Mr. Claghorn it was resolved that the building shall cover the whole lot and that the total furnished cost shall not exceed $200,000." Building to include "a Library and Directors' Room. | Lecture Room | Life Class Room | Antique, Linen Room | Lumber Room | Water Closets on each floor | Entresol rooms | Steam Heat | Apartments at both ends for Curator and Porter." BCM

JUNE 19, 1871 A letter to John Sartain from John Windrim requests more specifications for the competition. See I-004. CBC 1871–2 folder

NOVEMBER 13, 1871 The Building Committee reports that after the tie between Thomas Richards and Furness & Hewitt for first place in the competition, the committee has recommended the latter as the architects, and the board adopts the motion. BM 1865–74 (copied version in 1858–76), pp. 370–74

NOVEMBER 16, 1871 "The New Academy of Fine Arts" is announced in the press, "Messrs. Hewitt & Furness have been chosen as architects, under the direction of the Board. The interior has already been designed, and the plans have been published. The work on the new Academy will be commenced early in the spring." *Philadelphia Inquirer*, p. 2

DECEMBER 11, 1871 The Building Committee states that, as instructed by the board, F&H have been hired to act as architects to the Academy for the sum of $6,000, less $400 already paid as the premium for winning the competition. "For this they engage to prepare plans and drawings for the new Academy of the Fine Arts Building that shall be satisfactory to the Directors, will make full and complete working drawings, fully superintend and direct the construction of the building throughout to its final completion." Payment is conditional on the building being realized. BM1858–76, p. 376

JANUARY 4, 1872 Minutes of the Building Committee indicate adoption of the design, with the inclusion of the adjustments proposed by John Sartain; F&H (who were present) are "requested to prepare plans for the Academy building in general accordance therewith." BCM

APRIL 8, 1872 Committees on academy property and on the building (Rogers, Sartain, Gibson, Morris, Baird) are named. It is announced that subscriptions for the new building have reached $230,000. BM1858–76, pp. 396–99

MAY 13, 1872 The president announces that the time has arrived for "calling in five per cent of the subscriptions for the new Academy building," and proposes that "the Secretary issue notice at once that that installment would be due and payable on the 1st of June next. And it was so ordered." BM1858–76, pp. 400–402

MAY 16, 1872 The president states that the Building Committee has "opened the bids received from contractors for clearing away from the Academy's lot at the S.W. corner of Broad and Cherry Streets, all the building and material now on it, the cleaning and stacking of the materials, the digging out of the depth required by the walls up to the level of the surrounding surface." Jacob Myers is engaged as construction superintendent at a salary of $1,500 per annum, commencing on June 1. BM1858–76, pp. 402–3

JUNE 10, 1872 A formal ceremony to lay the cornerstone is proposed and it is agreed "that Mr. Horace Binney, the only survivor of the original founders of the Academy, be invited to officiate on that occasion, seconded and assisted by the late [prior] President, Mr. Caleb Cope. The ceremony to take place in the Fall of the year." BM1858–76, pp. 403–4

NOVEMBER 14, 1872 Steward & Stevens ironworks submits a proposal to furnish the iron beams for the first floor of the new building. Note at bottom: accepted by PAFA on November 19, with James Claghorn's name nearby. CBC 1871–2 folder

DECEMBER 7, 1872 The board members "proceed together to the South West corner of Broad and Cherry Streets and there participate in the Ceremony of laying the corner stone of the new Academy Building. The preparations had been already made by the Building Committee: the gentlemen who were to speak were notified, the objects to be placed in the cavity of the stone collected, and all necessary details connected with the exercises completed." BM1858–76, pp. 410–23

MARCH 10, 1873 The Building Committee report that "there have been four bids for the outside stonework of the academy building, the lowest of which was $52,550 and was that of Messrs. Atkinson and Myhlertz, to whom consequently the contract has been awarded." BM1858–76, pp. 431–32

JULY 14, 1873 Letter from Atkinson & Myhlertz to F&H notes that employees are on strike for higher wages, with the employers unwilling to give any ground. "If the strike should last longer than we expect, we will go down and set at the Academy ourselves, as most of the stuff is cut and ready for setting, so as to cause no delay, which we trust will be satisfactory." CBC 1873–4 folder

DECEMBER 8, 1873 Fairman Rogers reports on behalf of the Building Committee on the "present date of progress on the work at the new building, and that the walls were now nearly all covered in to protect them from the weather during the approaching winter." BM1858–76, pp. 443–44

APRIL 15, 1874 F&H are present at a meeting to consider the construction of the roof and approve estimates. It was "Resolved that the roof be of slate which was adopted unanimously." Bid of the Phoenix Iron Company—still the lowest bidder after other figures were submitted—was accepted. Bids were to be obtained from "Morris; Bement; Phoenix Company" for the iron brackets over the galleries. On the question of whether iron wire or lathe be used for the plaster of the cove of galleries, it was "Resolved that lath plaster on both sides be adopted. Unanimous. / Resolved that the wood as a material for floor be rejected." The material for the grand stairway was considered: the Natrona stone contracted for being unavailable, the architects recommended Berea stone "since marble cannot be had in single lengths." Berea stone was adopted with the understanding that the architects obtain a suitable reduction in cost from Mr. Struthers. BCM

JUNE 8, 1874 Building Committee chairman Rogers advises that "he was not quite sure whether the iron frame work for the roof was in actual progress, because it appeared that the contract for it had not yet been signed. That the building could probably be urged forward to completion by next Spring [1875], provided such progress was not too rapid a draft on the supplies in the Treasury." BM1858–76, pp. 453–56

SEPTEMBER 14, 1874 The president announces to the board the purchase for the Academy of "the lot of ground occupying the whole space on Broad Street between the new Academy Building and the Church at the North West corner of Broad and Arch Streets. It measures 71 feet on the Street front, by 147 feet in depth westward, and the cost was $55.000.-, of which $50.000. remains on Ground rent. It is extremely desirable that a right of way from the rear of it to the narrow street west of it obtained across what is now the Northern end of a garden to a house on Arch St., and it is believed that this may be purchased." The board approved this action. Claghorn also suggested that an exhibition be held in "the building" [he may be referring to the lot just purchased?] for the "benefit of the Academy." BM1858–76, pp. 457–59

MAY 1, 1875 The president states that the meeting has been convened "for the purpose of devising some way of providing money for carrying on the new building. It has been proposed to do this by borrowing from the Philadelphia Savings Fund Society on the mortgage held by the Academy on the Chestnut Street property purchased by Robert Fox

from the Academy." This motion was approved, with a $50,000 loan to be taken out (the mortgage was for $60,000). BM1858–76, pp. 470–71

SEPTEMBER 8, 1875 A letter from Fairman Rogers to John Sartain says: "My dear Sir: / I enclose a letter from Mr. Aspinwall about tile floors. I have no particular comment to make upon it as I believe that the cement or lithogen has been already decided upon, but I sent it for the information of the Committee." CBC 1875 folder

NOVEMBER 8, 1875 A letter from John Gibson to "Committee of Pa. Academy of The Fine Arts" says: "We will make rich Stained Ornamental Glass for Skylight of Main Stairway for designs submitted, Rich Ornamental Border and plain white ground glass Centre and glass the same." CBC 1875 folder

FEBRUARY 14, 1876 The board discusses whether the building will be ready to mount its first Spring Exhibition. "The President alluded to the opening of the first exhibition in the new building, and the expediency of so ordering it as to render the occasion as imposing as possible. With this view he had arranged with Mr. Theodore Cuyler to prepare and deliver an opening address, with Mr. Fairman Rogers chairman of the Building Committee, for such report and statements relative to the structure as would interest the audience in that particular." It was also stated that he proposed to "invite Artists from New York, and by all proper means to add to the éclat of the grand inauguration of the Academy's first display in its new home."

Frank Furness reports that, in accordance with instructions received from the president of the Academy, he has "spoken with Mr. [Alexander] Kemp, the Sculptor, and ascertained at what price he would carve the eight slabs of stone in the Academy front to represent as many groups in Delaroche's Hemicycle. That his price was $1200. for the entire work. After due consideration it was decided that the commission be given to Mr. Kemp on the terms named." BM1858–76, pp. 500–503

MAY 6, 1876 "Last week the society opened its new building . . . ," *American Architect and Building News* (PR box incl year 1876)

Installation of *Building a Masterpiece: Frank Furness's Factory for Art*, 2012, looking east from the rotunda

GEORGE E. THOMAS is a cultural and architectural historian who serves as co-director, with architect Susan Snyder, of the Critical Conservation program at Harvard's Graduate School of Design. He received his PhD from the University of Pennsylvania, where he taught between 1978 and 2014 in the Urban Studies and Historic Preservation programs (which he helped found in 1978). In 1995, he was awarded the University's Provost's Award for Distinguished Teaching.

Dr. Thomas's initial documentary research informed the Philadelphia Museum of Art's landmark 1973 exhibition, *The Architecture of Frank Furness*, transforming the perception of the architect as an oddball, known for a few radical projects, to that of a remarkable professional with as many as eight hundred commissions. Furness's stream of students—including Louis Sullivan and William L. Price—transformed American architecture along the lines that had been developed in his office. The present study of the construction of the Pennsylvania Academy of the Fine Arts continues Dr. Thomas's research into Furness and draws on a larger forthcoming study, *Inventing Modern: The Architecture of Frank Furness in an Age of Great Machines*, which situates the architect in the industrial culture that provided a theoretical basis for his work.

Dr. Thomas has written and lectured widely on nineteenth and early twentieth century American architecture, with a focus on the relationship between cultural innovation and architectural design. His books include *William L. Price: From Arts and Crafts to Modern Design* (2000); and, as co-author, *Cape May: Queen of the Seaside Resorts* (1976), with Carl Doebley; *Drawing Toward Building: Philadelphia Architectural Graphics 1732–1986* (1986), with James F. O'Gorman, Jeffrey A. Cohen, and G. Holmes Perkins; *Frank Furness: The Complete Works* (1990, revised edition 1996), with Michael J. Lewis and Jeffrey A. Cohen; *Building America's First University: An Architectural and Historical Guide to the University of Pennsylvania* (2000), with David B. Brownlee; and *Buildings of Pennsylvania: Philadelphia and Eastern Pennsylvania* (2010), with Patricia Ricci, Richard Webster, Lawrence Newman, Robert Janosev, and J. Bruce Thomas.

In addition to his academic work, he is a co-founder, also with Susan Snyder, of CivicVisions, a multi-disciplinary research and consulting firm whose research methodologies combine an understanding of a place's history with the ability to create a future that responds to contemporary lifestyle forces.

PHOTOGRAPHY CREDITS

In reproducing images contained in this publication, every effort has been made to identify rights holders and obtain permission for use. Errors or omissions in credit citations have been either unavoidable or unintentional. In those instances where rights holders could not be located, notwithstanding good faith efforts, the author and publisher welcome any information that would allow them to correct future reprints.

The Academy of Natural Sciences of Drexel University: fig. 78. **Athenaeum of Philadelphia**: figs. 55: *The Official Office Building Directory and Architectural Handbook of Philadelphia* (Philadelphia: The Commercial Publishing and Directory Co., 1899); 90: Theophilus Parsons Chandler, Elevation, School and Studio Building for the Pennsylvania Academy of the Fine Arts, CHN.005.002. **Baker Library, Harvard Business School**: pp. 40–41: Trade Catalog Collection, Baldwin Locomotive Works, Philadelphia, *Exhibit at the World's Columbian Exposition, Chicago 1893*. **Boston Public Library**: figs. 47: Museum of Fine Arts, Boston, Copley Square, c. 1876–95, albumen print, 08_02_002785; 87: Trinity Church, c. 1875, derived from stereograph, 06_11_000040, America Illustrated, Boston & Suburbs. **Bryn Mawr College Special Collections**: fig. 43. ©**City of Philadelphia**: fig. 36: Department of Records, 11936-0-7813. **Denver Art Museum**: fig. 32: William Sr. and Dorothy Harmsen Collection, by exchange, 2008.490. **Esto**: figs. 1: ©Ezra Stoller/Esto; 3: ©Jeff Goldberg/Esto; 12: ©David Sundberg/Esto; 14: ©Lara Swimmer/Esto. **Free Library of Philadelphia/Bridgeman Images**: fig. 40: Center Square, site of City Hall, c. 1875, albumen print, Historical Images of Philadelphia collection—Castner Scrapbook Collection, Samuel Castner, compiler; pp. 18: Centennial Photographic Co., (*top*) The Lake—Centennial grounds, 1876, silver albumen print, Photographic Services I; (*bottom*) Machinery Hall, transept, from north end, 1876, silver albumen print, Photographic Services II; 80: North Broad Street from City Hall, c. 1871, albumen print, Historical Images of Philadelphia collection, Robert Newell, photographer. **Hagley Museum and Library**: fig. 84: Lawrence S. Williams, Inc. photographer, 1970/1989, PSFS Photograph Collection, 1993.302, 93302_box6_026. **Zachary Hartzell**: pp. 106–107, 116–117, 120 (*bottom*), 121. **Haverford College Library**: fig. 49: Quaker Collection, Addison Hutton papers, Coll. no. 1122, Diaries, 1870–1915. ©2013 **Kimbell Art Museum**: fig. 4: Robert LaPrelle, photographer. **Isaac Kornblatt-Stier**: fig. 13. **Michael J. Lewis**: p. 14 (*bottom*). **Library of Congress**: figs. 35: Keystone View Co., publisher, c. 1905, stereograph; 53B: Historic American Building Survey, Jack E. Boucher, photographer, HABS.PA.51-PHILA.344-1; 65: Historic American Building Survey, Robert Harris, photographer, HABS.PA.51-PHILA.326; 68: Historic American Building Survey, HABS.PA.51-PHILA.405–17; 84: Traymore Hotel, Atlantic City, New Jersey, c. 1920, Irving Underhill, photographer. ©**Maryland Historical Society**: fig. 34: Baltimore City Life Museum Collection; Museum Department, MA5911. **National Academy of Design/Bridgeman Images**: fig. 44. **Pennsylvania Academy of the Fine Arts**: Dorothy and Kenneth Woodcock Archives at PAFA: figs. 11A–B, 41, 46, 50A–B, 64, 81–83, 91A–B, 92, 94; pp. 58, 62, 96–97, 111, 124; Day & Zimmermann Associates: figs. 66, 86; Harris & Davis Photography: fig. 62; pp. 11 (*top*); 76–77, 92–93, 102–103; Rick Echelmeyer: fig. 20; Barbara Katus: figs. 5: Bequest of Dr. Paul J. Sartain, 1948.23.30; 6: Gift of Horace Howard Furness, 1899.8; 7B, 9, 10, 15, 16: 1876.6.27; 17, 18A–C, 19, 26, 27, 30: 1876.6.28; 31: Gift of Charles Henry Hart, 1893.5.8; 33: Joseph E. Temple Fund, 1894.4; 37, 38: Gift of Mrs. James L. Claghorn, 1884.3; 39: 1956.41a; 42: Through the generosity of its dedicated supporters, ©Claes Oldenburg, *Paint Torch*, 2011; Plinth sculpture: ©Robert Taplin, *The Young Punch Juggling*, 2014. 51: 1876.6.12; 52: 1876.6.17a; 54, 57:1876.6.4; 58: 1876.6.30a; 59: 1876.6.30b; 60: 1876.6.18; 61: 1876.6.26; 63, 71, 72: 1876.6.10; 73: 1876.6.3; 74A: 1876.6.15b; 74B: 1876.6.15b; 75, 79, 80; pp. 4–5, 6–7, 27, 34: Gift of the Lyon Family, 1842.1; 38: Joseph E. Temple Fund, 1894.4; 44–47, 50: Funds provided by an Anonymous donor, 1990.15; 58, 60, 61: 1876.6.8; 68–69, 72: (*top: detail*) 1876.6.30a, (*middle: detail*) 1876.6.30b; 86–87, 100, 118–119, 122, jacket front and back. **Lewis Tanner**: figs. 44, 67, 69. **Temple University Libraries**, **Special Collections Research Center**: fig. 93: William Owens, photographer, architect Hyman Myers, Philadelphia Evening Bulletin, George D. McDowell Philadelphia Evening Bulletin Collection, SCRC170. **George E. Thomas**: figs. 7A, 21A–B, 22–24, 28, 53A, 70, 76; frontispiece, pp. 9: Coca Cola®; 11 (*bottom*); 52: Constitutional Centennial Celebration, Industrial Parade, North Broad Street, Philadelphia, September 15, 1887, gift of George E. Thomas to PAFA; 54, 120 (*top*). **University of Pennsylvania, Architectural Archives and Pennsylvania Historical and Museum Commission: Louis I. Kahn Collection**: figs. 28, 88: photographer, Malcolm Smith. **University of Pennsylvania, University Archives and Records Center**: figs. 48, 77, 78; p. 14 (*top*). **Venturi, Scott Brown and Associates Inc.**: figs. 2, 29: David Hirsch, photographer; 88. **Victoria and Albert Museum**: fig. 8: John Absolon (1815–1895), Lloyd Brothers & Co., publishers, General view, Crystal Palace, 1851, lithograph, colored by hand, 19538:2.

PAFA
Pennsylvania Academy
of the Fine Arts

Library of Congress Cataloging-in-Publication Data

Names: Thomas, George E., author.
Title: First modern : Pennsylvania Academy of the Fine Arts / George E. Thomas.
Description: Philadelphia : Pennsylvania Academy of the Fine Arts, 2017. |
  Includes bibliographical references.
Identifiers: LCCN 2017018720 | ISBN 9780943836430 (hardcover : alk. paper)
Subjects: LCSH: Pennsylvania Academy of the Fine Arts. | Furness, Frank,
  1839-1912. | Hewitt, George Watson, 1841-1916. | Art museum
  architecture--Pennsylvania--Philadelphia--History--19th century. | Art
  schools--Pennsylvania--Philadelphia--History--19th century. | Architecture
  and society--Pennsylvania--Philadelphia--History--19th century. |
  Philadelphia (Pa.)--Buildings, structures, etc.
Classification: LCC N680 .T49 2017 | DDC 727/.70974811--dc23
LC record available at https://lccn.loc.gov/2017018720

Published by Pennsylvania Academy of the Fine Arts, Philadelphia
www.pafa.org

Distributed by University of Pennsylvania Press
www.upenn.edu/pennpress

Produced by Lucia|Marquand, Seattle
www.luciamarquand.com

Edited by L. Jane Calverley and Judith M. Thomas
PAFA production managed by Judith M. Thomas
Designed by Susan E. Kelly
Typeset in Alright Sans by Susan E. Kelly
Proofread by Ted Gilley, Laurel McLaughlin, and Judith M. Thomas
Color management by iocolor, Seattle
Printed and bound in China by Artron Art Group